Activism, Burnout, and Community in Higher Education

This illuminating volume explores the often-overlooked relationship between college student activism and well-being, drawing on a multi-phase study that explores college students' perspectives on how their activism impacts their well-being.

Based on a study of 119 US college students, the authors share their findings through a constructivist, qualitative lens, revealing three key themes: The link between student activism and students' identities, the non-negotiable time costs of activism and associated burnout, and the ways that students and higher education can benefit from a different way of considering university and community care. With scholarship exploring the connections between college student activism and well-being still nascent, this book pioneers a fresh understanding of the intersection between student activism and well-being, amplifying authentic student voices throughout and offering practical recommendations for student support. Through a combination of personal narratives, data analysis, and expert commentary, it explores what inspires college student activists to work to create a more just and equitable society, as well as the prevalence of burnout and the tools students use to mitigate their struggles and improve their own well-being.

This book will be suitable for both undergraduate and graduate students as well as scholars, practitioners, and professionals in the larger higher education and social justice community.

Cher Weixia Chen is Associate Professor in the School of Integrative Studies at George Mason University, USA.

Graziella Pagliarulo McCarron is Associate Professor in the School of Integrative Studies at George Mason University, USA.

Julie E. Owen is Associate Professor in the School of Integrative Studies at George Mason University, USA.

Steve Grande is Assistant Professor of Graduate Psychology and Program Director of the College Student Personnel Administration program at James Madison University, USA.

Routledge Research in Higher Education

Experiential Learning and Community Partnerships for Sustainable Development
A Foundational Model for Climate Action
Mara Huber, Michael Jabot, and Christina Heath

Philosophical Adventures in African Higher Education
Cultivating Doctoral Encounters within Democratic Citizenship Education
Edited by Yusef Waghid

Developing Feedback Literacy for Academic Journal Peer Review
Narratives from Researchers in Education and Applied Linguistics
Edited by Sin Wang Chong and Aurora Lixinhao Gao

Exploring Research Impact in Academia and Why it Matters
Perspectives on the Public Good and the Role of Research in Society
Andy Phippen and Louise Rutt

Learning Analytics for Achieving Quality Assurance in Higher Learning Institutions
Malaysian Perspectives for Global Insights
Soo Mang Lim and Husaina Banu Kenayathulla

For more information about this series, please visit: www.routledge.com/Routledge-Research-in-Higher-Education/book-series/RRHE

Activism, Burnout, and Community in Higher Education

Narratives of College Student Activists

Cher Weixia Chen,
Graziella Pagliarulo McCarron,
Julie E. Owen, and Steve Grande

NEW YORK AND LONDON

First published 2025
by Routledge
605 Third Avenue, New York, NY 10158

and by Routledge
4 Park Square, Milton Park, Abingdon, Oxon, OX14 4RN

Routledge is an imprint of the Taylor & Francis Group, an informa business

ISBN: 9781032767031 (hbk)
ISBN: 9781032770499 (pbk)
ISBN: 9781003481010 (ebk)

DOI: 10.4324/9781003481010

Typeset in Times New Roman
by Newgen Publishing UK

To

the student activists who tirelessly strive to create positive social change.

Contents

Acknowledgments

This book is a testament to the power of friendship. As authors from diverse disciplinary backgrounds and two institutions, we came together with a shared passion for research, activism, student development, and well-being. The journey began at a conference, where Cher had a conversation with an activist who confided, "activism is lonely." This statement struck her like a lightning bolt, sparking the inspiration for this project. Fortunately, friends and colleagues soon joined her, transforming this effort into one of the most rewarding experiences of our lives.

We are deeply grateful to the student activists whose love and labor are changing the world: You are the heartbeat of this work. We also extend our thanks to the scholars and practitioners whose work has inspired and scaffolded this volume.

A special thank you goes to the students who provided research assistance: Dina Rachel Berenshteyn, Sarah Blanton, Gabriella Guerrieri, Rafaela Gonzalez Lucioni, Ellen Gurung, Anagha Sreevals, Jasmin Enciu, Jordan April, Isabella LaMagdeleine, Cristal Badu, Brenda Lynn Goodson, Rafaela Gonzalez Lucioni, Kendall Reed Cage, and Mireya Katherine Campuzano. We also wish to express our gratitude to the following colleagues who have been integral to this journey and project: Xiaomei Cai, Taimi Castle, Melody Porter, and Lisa Lynn Porter.

We appreciate the funding provided by the George Mason University Office of Student Creative Activities and Research Summer Impact Project Grant and the 4-VA Collaborative Research Grant.

Cher would like to extend heartfelt thanks to her wonderful friends, Graziella, Julie, and Steve—what an amazing journey we have had together! She also expresses deep gratitude to her immediate family,

Shawn and Ivy, for their understanding and support during the many nights she spent writing.

Graziella shares her deepest thanks with her incredible co-authors and dear friends, Cher, Julie, and Steve—working with you all on this volume has been a gift. Graziella also thanks her immediate family (Keith and sweet Oliver) as well as her larger family and loving community.

Julie thanks, first and foremost, her generous and generative co-authors, for their ongoing support, collaboration, and treasured friendship. The opportunity to work together on this project was so meaningful. Thank you also to her family (Connie, Ken, Laura, and Bennett) and fur family (*feles catus magnum et modicum*, also known as Max and Minnie).

Steve feels such a debt of gratitude to Cher, Graziella, and Julie for the invitation to collaborate on this project. Their intellect, compassion, sense of humor, and authenticity has made a lasting impact on his practice. This is important work and they each brought joy, mentorship, dedication, and patience (with me). Steve sends his love and thanks to Sweetie Pie.

1 Introduction to Activism, Burnout, and Community

According to Couch (2004), "activist" can be described as "a role assumed by individuals or collective actors either to resist what they consider to be a political wrong or to bring about political change, through contained or transgressive tactics" (p. 15). Such a form of politically oriented activism has its origins in the concept of a "Jeffersonian democracy" (Miller & Nadler, 2018), emphasizing the importance of advocacy among Americans for themselves and their communities. While the historical dynamics of who had the privilege of enacting such changes have been subject to debate, for those empowered through a combination of authority and identity, participation in activism has served as a means of influencing decision-makers to effect social change; it serves as a form of "demand making" (Miller & Nadler, 2018, p. 3).

Over time, the phenomenon of "demand-making" has evolved to encompass broader social issues beyond the political sphere, reaching universities and colleges. As aptly demonstrated in Boren's (2019) *Student resistance: A history of the unruly subject*, which traces the trajectory of student movements in the U.S. from their earliest documented occurrences to the contemporary movements they have inspired within and beyond the confines of academia, activism/demand-making has become deeply ingrained in university culture as both an intra- and extra-institutional driver of change. In fact, throughout history, college student activism has remained a consistent and integral element in the narrative of higher education, threading its way through periods of peace, conflict, political upheaval, community transformation, and calls for equity. In their comprehensive examination, Miller and Nadler (2018) analyzed the multifaceted nature of

DOI: 10.4324/9781003481010-1

college student activism, highlighting how "college-aged students have typically been among the most sensitive to societal issues and subsequently, among the vocal and active in seeking change and recognition" (p. 2).

Interestingly, despite a perceived dormancy in the late 1990s and early 2000s, there has been a notable resurgence of student activism both in the U.S. and internationally over the past decade, as highlighted by Baker and Blissett (2018) and Cole and Heinecke (2020). This resurgence coincides with the persistent manifestation of historical injustices. A report by the Education Advisory Board (EAB) (Cudé, 2020) examining student activism between 2015 and 2020 across universities in the U.S., Europe, Canada, and South Africa, underscores this trend. The report identifies a sharp increase in student demands for change, a growing urgency for expeditious issue resolution, and a preference for accountability over negotiation. Notably, the three primary foci of student activism during this period were racial justice, political events, and university responses to COVID-19. This observation aligns with Jacoby's (2017) perspective on universities as microcosms of larger societal dynamics, emphasizing the significant role students play not only in instigating campus reforms, but also in driving broader systemic changes.

The resurgence of student activism on university campuses is vividly demonstrated through various initiatives, including, among others, multicultural movements, graduate student unionization, desegregation, international, and social inclusion movements (Rhoads, 2009). This activism, which takes shape both in person and online—via platforms like social media and forms of digital engagement known as "clicktivism" (Akhlaghpour & Vaast, 2018) and sometimes derided as "slacktivism" (Cabrera, 2017)—plays a pivotal role in giving voice to previously unheard perspectives. The significance of student-led groups in fostering dialogue and action is underscored by Kozuma (2015), who observed the transformative power of student organization coalitions in amplifying individual and collective voices, stating, "they have served as vehicles for students … to empower their individual and collective voices" (p. iv). Such activism is crucial in the pursuit of social justice, which involves challenging the prevailing economic and social norms to achieve genuine equity for everyone (Rhoads, 2009).

While there is a growing understanding of the institutional effects and various dimensions of college student activism, there remains a gap in our knowledge concerning how activists themselves view the relationship between their activism and other elements of their lives. One element that is markedly understudied is well-being. Amidst the renewed vigor of student activism and the existing research gap on the connection between activism and well-being, our study aims to contribute to the literature on college student activism. From the perspectives of 119 U.S. college student activists, our research explored the complex dynamics between college student activists' engagement in activism and their sense of well-being. Utilizing a constructivist, qualitative approach via individual interviews, the study investigated the experiences of college student activists, seeking to broaden the discourse and pinpoint opportunities for improved support.

The central research question driving our inquiry was *How do college student activists perceive their activism, well-being, and the relation between the two?* This investigation aimed to amplify the voices of college student activists, paving the way for developing practical strategies that nurture their well-being. The study specifically sought to understand how student activists defined well-being, how they perceived the interplay between their activism's benefits, costs, and well-being, and how, if at all, they experienced burnout.

Significance of This Work

Several key factors speak to the significance of this volume:

- This book is grounded in an empirical study, framed by an interpretive, constructivist qualitative design, which shared the voices of college student activists working to effect social change. Drawing on 119 interviews of college student activists, this book provides a comprehensive and nuanced view of the motivations, challenges, and strategies associated with their activism. In offering students' stories, we recognize the complexity and diversity within the "activist" identity, acknowledging that terms like "advocate" or "organizer" might resonate more with some. Although we use "activist" in our writing, reflecting its common usage in student change-making literature (Linder et al., 2019), we encourage readers to interpret it as a conceptual representation rather than a fixed label.

- The book features a range of college student activists from varied backgrounds and political perspectives, including those involved in issues such as racial justice, women's rights, immigration rights, LGBTQ+ rights, environmental sustainability, and economic inequality. Through their lenses, readers will gain insight into what inspires college student activists to work to create a more just and equitable society, as well as the prevalence of burnout, and the tools they use to address their struggles and improve their own well-being.
- This text offers a platform for student voices. It also provides critical analysis and commentary from the perspectives of fields such as social justice and human rights, leadership studies, and higher education. By situating the stories of student activists within broader social and political contexts, this book offers a deeper understanding of the impact and potential of college student activism.

Theoretical Underpinnings

Our study employed a constructivist approach to prioritize the lived experiences of participants, exploring their diverse perspectives through the lens of both positive and negative experiences. We utilized Diener's (2009) conceptual framework of Subjective Well-Being (SWB) to anchor our investigation. Maddux (2018) describes SWB as a psychological concept that centers on individuals' evaluations and emotional responses to their life conditions, rather than the external conditions themselves. This concept encompasses both affective aspects, such as emotions and feelings, and cognitive components, including judgments of life satisfaction, thus recognizing the range of positive and negative experiences (Diener, 2009; Maddux, 2018). Given the prevalence of mental health concerns among student activists, investigating SWB is crucial. It not only aids in comprehending their overall well-being, but also serves as a foundation for creating targeted support interventions that address their specific needs (Keyes, 2006). SWB provides a multifaceted evaluation of an individual's life, comprising four interrelated components: Pleasant emotions, unpleasant emotions, global life judgments, and domain satisfaction. Per Table 1.1, these components encompass sub-components that span across emotional states, life evaluations, and levels of satisfaction in different life domains.

Table 1.1 Subjective Well-Being Components and Sample Sub-Components

Pleasant Emotions	*Unpleasant Emotions*	*Life Judgments*	*Domain Satisfaction*
Joy	Sadness	Life satisfaction	Marriage
Contentment	Anger	Fulfillment	Work
Happiness	Worry	Meaning	Health
Love	Stress	Success	Leisure

Note: Adapted from Diener and colleagues (2009).

The SWB framework served as a guide for our study, offering language to articulate the complex interplay between the activism efforts of college students and their overall well-being. By integrating SWB into our analytical framework, we aimed to capture a broad spectrum of student experiences, acknowledging the intricate dynamics of their activist work and its impact on their psychological and emotional states. This approach enabled us to explore the nuanced ways in which activism influences students' sense of happiness, fulfillment, and satisfaction, as well as the challenges and stressors college student activists face.

Our analytical and discussion phases are guided by an inclusive approach, considering not only the components of SWB as conceptualized by Diener (2009), but also participants' perspectives. This open-mindedness toward student experiences underlines our commitment to a holistic view of activism's impact on well-being. It recognizes that student activism is not a monolithic experience but a complex interplay of factors that can enhance or detract from students' sense of well-being.

Research Design

Positionality

Our research team is comprised of four faculty members and a dedicated group of undergraduate and graduate researchers. Among the faculty, three have a profound focus on student care and community, while the fourth is a staunch advocate for activists' wellness. The student researchers bring diverse experiences in championing causes like women's rights, racial justice, and immigration rights, with one using journalism as a tool for enduring societal change. Each team member entered this work with a deep commitment to student care, a significant understanding of the challenges and risks faced by student activists, and, in some cases, personal experiences of declining well-being due to activism and/or advocacy efforts.

Our study's primary aim was to examine how college student activists perceived and articulated their activism, alongside its potential benefits, costs, risks, and impacts on their well-being. In line with Merriam and Tisdell (2016), we employed an interpretive, constructivist qualitative study design. This approach is geared toward comprehending participants' subjective interpretations of their experiences and how they shape their realities, ensuring a nuanced and empathetic exploration of their lived experiences.

Settings and Participants

Since 2019, our research team has been gathering narratives from college student activists across 12 varied institutions in the mid-Atlantic region of the U.S. These institutions were thoughtfully selected to provide a wide representation in terms of geography, size, setting, and affiliation. Mindful of the literature highlighting the particular vulnerabilities of student activists from minoritized groups, we intentionally incorporated minority-serving institutions into our selection. Embracing a constructivist approach with reference to Merriam and Tisdell (2016), our research created a space for participants to articulate and interpret their experiences in their own terms.

In the process of participant recruitment, we utilized purposeful sampling techniques, identifying participants through both formal and informal networks, consistent with the snowball sampling method outlined by Creswell and Creswell (2018). We disseminated study invitations across relevant social media platforms and listservs, reached out to students in various campus organizations, and encouraged participants to recommend peers. Our inclusion criteria were as follows: (a) enrollment as a full-time or part-time student at the institution, whether graduate or undergraduate; (b) 18 years of age or older; and (c) engagement in activism, as self-defined by each participant. Our goal was to avoid imposing a predefined concept of "activism" on participants, thereby broadening the scope for participation. True to our constructivist perspective, we embraced an open definition of "activism," recognizing the diversity within the "activist" identity and allowing for a wider range of student experiences.

Our study encompassed 119 participants, spanning from first-year to doctoral students, who identified with multiple and intersecting identities. The spectrum of activism among the participants was broad, touching upon issues such as labor rights, gender equality, food insecurity, homelessness, educational equity, children's rights, veterans' rights, LGBTQ+ rights, environmental justice, the de-corporatization of higher education, racism, and immigrant rights. Table 1.2 provides a detailed summary of the self-reported characteristics of our participants.

Data Collection

Our data collection process, designed to complement our constructivist approach, consisted of individual, semi-structured interviews, allowing students to articulate their experiences authentically (Charmaz, 2014). This methodology received approval from our Institutional Review Board to ensure ethical standards. Conducted in person or online, each interview lasted up to one hour. Participants were given informed consent documents beforehand, detailing their rights to withdraw from the study at any time and outlining the measures taken to ensure confidentiality and data security.

The interview questions were developed from relevant literature and refined through expert pilot reviews by faculty engaged in student activist research. These inquiries probe the motivations behind students' activism and the support systems and challenges students encounter. The interviews were carried out by our research team after extensive training on best practices with respect to interviewing, rapport-building, and safe space holding. To maintain anonymity, interviews were recorded, transcribed verbatim to preserve voice, and participants were either given or chose pseudonyms to protect their identity.

Data Analysis and Trustworthiness

Data analyses were conducted concurrently with data collection through a method of constant comparison (Jones et al., 2013), allowing for an iterative process between conducting interviews and analyzing data, in keeping with constructivist principles (Creswell & Poth, 2017). This

Table 1.2 Participant Self-Reported Demographics and Activism Details (N=119)

Pseudonym	*Gender ID*	*Racial ID*	*Age*	*Time as Activist*	*Activism Focus*
Aaliyah	Woman	Black	20	4–6 years	Racial Justice; Health Equity
Abigail	Woman	White	21	Less than 1 yr	Sexual Violence & Women's Rights
Alanis	Woman	Black	19	4–6 years	Racial Justice
Alexis	Woman	Latina	20	Less than 1 yr	Criminal Justice Reform
Allison	Woman	Black	25	Less than 1 yr	Racial Justice; LGBTQ+ Rights; Immigrant Rights
Amanda	Woman	Latina	21	4–6 years	Sexual Violence & Women's Rights
Andrea	Woman	White	20	4–6 years	Women's Rights; Racial Justice; Immigrant & Refugee Rights
Angie	Woman	White	22	1–3 years	Sexual Violence; Higher Education Transparency
Anna F.	Non-Binary	White	20	1–3 years	Environmental Justice
Anna R.	Woman	South Asian	19	1–3 years	Food Insecurity
Apranik	Woman	Middle Eastern	19	1–3 years	Racial Justice
Ashley	Woman	Latina	21	4–6 years	Immigrant Rights
Audrey	Woman	White	25	7–9 years	Sexual Violence
Axel	Non-Binary	White	20	1–3 years	Racial Justice
Benjamin	Non-Binary	White	22	7–9 years	LGBTQ+ Rights; Politics and Policy
Bethany	Woman	White	22	4–6 years	Women's Rights
Billie	Non-Binary	White	19	Less than 1 yr	Housing Rights
Bob	Man	White	22	4–6 years	Education
Cal	Non-Binary	White	19	1–3 years	Racial Justice; LGBTQ+ Rights; Sexual Violence

Cameron	Woman	Asian	21	1–3 years	Cultural Awareness
Catherine	Woman	White	20	4–6 years	Women's Rights; Gun Violence
Cheryl	Woman	White	20	4–6 years	Political Rights & Inclusion
Chloe	Woman	Latina	21	1–3 years	Food Insecurity
Chrissy	Woman	White	27	1–3 years	Graduate & Professional Student Rights
Christina	Woman	Black	22	1–3 years	Education Equity & Transparency
Clara C.	Woman	Latina	23	4–6 years	Immigrant Rights
Clara V.	Woman	Latina	21	4–6 years	Immigrant Rights
Daisy	Woman	White	19	1–3 years	Nutrition; Health
Dana	Woman	White	40	20+ years	Education; Veteran Advocacy
Daphne	Woman	Cameroonian-American	19	Less than 1 yr	Environmental Justice & Racism
David C.	Man	Black	21	10+ years	Immigrant Rights; Environmental Justice
David P.	Man	White	27	10+ years	Racial Justice
Denise	Woman	White	20	1–3 years	Environmental Justice
Destiny D.	Woman	Black	19	1–3 years	Women's Rights
Destiny W.	Woman	White	22	4–6 years	Disability Rights & Accessibility
Dion	Man	Latino	23	4–6 years	Immigrant Rights; LGBTQ+ Rights; Voting Rights
Edith	Woman	White	20	4–6 years	Disability Rights & Accessibility
Elena	Woman	White	20	1–3 years	Sexual Violence; Women's Rights
Elijah	Man	Black & White	21	4–6 years	Disability Rights & Accessibility
Eliza A.	Woman	White	21	1–3 years	Sexual Violence & Women's Rights
Eliza M.	Woman	Latina	20	1–3 years	Diversity & Inclusion
Elizabeth	Woman	South Asian & White	21	1–3 years	LGBTQ+ Rights; Racial Justice; Health/Disability Justice

(Continued)

Table 1.2 (Continued)

Pseudonym	*Gender ID*	*Racial ID*	*Age*	*Time as Activist*	*Activism Focus*
Ellen	Woman	Asian	20	4–6 years	Reproductive Rights
Ely	Man	White	20	1–3 years	Food Insecurity
Emilia	Woman	South Asian	20	Less than 1 yr	Mental Health
Emily	Woman	Latina	22	1–3 years	Criminal Justice Reform
Esther	Woman	White	30	1–3 years	Environmental Justice
Eugene	Man	White	18	4–6 years	Gun Violence; LGBTQ+ Rights
Evelyn	No Response	Asian	20	Less than 1 yr	Mental Health
Gabriella	Woman	Asian	20	Less than 1 yr	Asian American Activism; Sexual Health Education
George	Man	White	23	4–6 years	Higher Education Transparency
Giada	Woman	Asian & White	20	1–3 years	Labor Rights
Grace	Woman	White	20	1–3 years	Environmental Justice
Haley	Woman	White	21	4–6 years	Children with Terminal Illness
Hannah H.	Woman	Middle Eastern	23	4–6 years	Pro-Palestinian Advocacy
Hannah R.	Woman	White	19	10+ years	Human Rights
Helen	Transfeminine	White	21	1–3 years	Higher Education Transparency
Illio	Man	Black	18	1–3 years	Political Rights & Inclusion
Jack	Man	Latino	20	1–3 years	Immigrant Rights
Jacob	Man	White & Jewish	28	7–9 years	Racial Justice; Environmental Justice
Jacqueline	Woman	Black, White, & Native American	20	1–3 years	Reproductive Rights; Indigenous Rights
Jada	Woman	Black	22	Less than 1 yr	Racial Justice; Student Rights
Jason	Man	Asian	20	1–3 years	Environmental Justice
Jay	Man	Asian	19	1–3 years	Asian American Activism

Jennifer G.	Woman	White	21	4–6 years	Education Equity & Transparency
Jennifer T.	Woman	White	22	Less than 1 yr	Higher Education Transparency
Jillian	Woman	Asian & White	20	1–3 years	Reproductive Rights
Joanne	Woman	Latina	22	4–6 years	Women's Rights; Immigrant & Refugee Rights
Johnson	Man	Black	20	4–6 years	Racial Justice & Police Reform
Joseph	Non-Binary	White	18	1–3 years	Racial Justice; Immigrant Rights
Julianne	Woman	Black	20	Less than 1 yr	Racial Justice; Women's Rights
Kara	Woman	White	22	4–6 years	Social Displacement
Karen	Woman	Latina & White	21	1–3 years	Environmental Justice
Kelsey	Woman	Asian	21	1–3 years	Racial Justice; Environmental Justice; Food Insecurity
Kimora	Woman	Black	23	1–3 years	Racial Justice; LGBTQ+ Rights; Women's Rights
Kyle	Man	Black	21	1–3 years	Racial Justice
Laura A.	Woman	Latina & White	22	1–3 years	Labor Rights; Higher Education Transparency
Laura G.	No Response	South Asian	20	4–6 years	Global South Advocacy
Lawrence	Man	White	23	4–6 years	Racial Justice; Immigrant Rights; Gender Equity
Layla	Woman	Black & White	22	1–3 years	Environmental Justice
Leah	Woman	White	21	4–6 years	Reproductive Rights
Liam	Man	Black	21	4–6 years	Foster Care Equity
Lily	Woman	White	20	4–6 years	Menstrual Equity; Power-Based Violence
Lucy	Woman	White	21	1–3 years	LGBTQ+ Rights
Luke	Man	White	21	1–3 years	Constitutional Rights
Madeleine	Woman	Asian & White	19	1–3 years	Civil Rights; Racial Justice; LGBTQ+ Rights
Madison	Woman	White	18	4–6 years	Women's Rights; Student Rights
Marcus	Non-Binary	Latinx	25	4–6 years	Sexual Violence; Women's Rights

(*Continued*)

Table 1.2 (Continued)

Pseudonym	*Gender ID*	*Racial ID*	*Age*	*Time as Activist*	*Activism Focus*
Marilyn	Woman	White	22	4–6 years	Political Rights & Inclusion
Marta	Woman	White	20	4–6 years	Human Rights
Mary A.	Woman	Latina	22	1–3 years	Racial Justice; Immigrant Rights
Mary J.	Woman	White	21	4–6 years	Racial Justice; Health Equity
Masvusi	Man	White	19	4–6 years	Gun Violence; LGBTQ+ Rights
Melissa K.	Woman	Middle Eastern	23	1–3 years	Environmental Justice
Melissa M.	Woman	White & Latina	23	Less than 1 yr	Immigrant & Child Rights
Michele	Woman	White	20	1–3 years	LGBTQ+ Rights; Racial Justice
Monica	Woman	Middle Eastern	19	1–3 years	Racial Justice
Monika	Woman	Black	21	1–3 years	Labor Rights
Naomi	Woman	White	21	4–6 years	Reproductive Rights; Women's Rights; LGBTQ+ Rights
Natalie	Woman	South Asian	21	1–3 years	Unhoused Individuals' Rights
Olivia	Woman	Latina	21	4–6 years	Immigrant Rights
Omar	Man	Latino	22	4–6 years	Student Rights
Patrick	Man	Asian	20	Less than 1 yr	Women's Rights; Racial Justice; LGBTQ+ Rights
Penny	Woman	Latina	19	4–6 years	Immigrant Rights; Racial Justice
Phil	Man	Latino	29	1–3 years	Marginalized Student Populations
Phoebe	Woman	Black	20	4–6 years	Racial Justice & Civil Rights
Rosa	Woman	Asian	21	1–3 years	Reproductive Rights
Shane	Man	Asian	18	Less than 1 yr	Health Equity
Shauna	Woman	Latina	19	1–3 years	Latinx Equity & Inclusion

Shay	Woman	Black	21	1–3 years	Racial Justice; LGBTQ+ Rights; Women's Rights
Sherry	Woman	Black	19	1–3 years	Racial Justice; Immigrant Rights
Sofia	Woman	White	21	1–3 years	Animal Rights
Stevie	Woman	South Asian	19	4–6 years	Women's Rights
Susan	Woman	White	21	1–3 years	Higher Education Transparency
Suvali	Woman	South Asian	25	1–3 years	Racial Justice; Women's Rights
Thomas	Man	White	22	4–6 years	Sexual Violence; LGBTQ+ Rights
Veronica	Woman	South Asian	21	1–3 years	Mental Health
Violet	Woman	Latina	20	1–3 years	Latinx Equity & Inclusion
Yasmine	Woman	Latina	21	4–6 years	Immigrant Rights

approach enabled us to navigate the complexities of the data and determine the point at which further collection and analysis could cease. Rather than adhering strictly to the concept of "data saturation," which suggests a finite amount of data can fully represent a phenomenon, we embraced Sims and Cilliers's (2023) perspective on achieving conceptual depth and prioritizing the richness and quality of the data.

Analysis began with a team of researchers performing broad, open coding (Corbin & Strauss, 2007) of the verbatim interview transcripts, which amounted to over 1640 pages of single-spaced text, alongside researcher notes. In line with triangulation practices (Glesne, 2016), the team collectively reviewed emerging themes to pinpoint similarities and differences. Themes ultimately shaped into broader categories, maintaining a focus on participant voices and ensuring analytical rigor by considering both common and "discrepant or negative cases" (Merriam & Tisdell, 2016, p. 259).

In our pursuit of ensuring the trustworthiness of our study, we followed Glesne's (2016) guidelines by implementing both method triangulation, utilizing diverse data collection methods such as interviews and field notes, and investigator triangulation, which involved engaging multiple researchers in discussions to identify both consensus and variance in findings. Further enhancing our study's credibility, we incorporated member-checking by sharing our analytical insights with participants for validation, conducted peer debriefing sessions with subject matter experts, and regularly reflected on our research processes. These reflections served as a basis for team discussions and were essential elements of our audit trail.

Structure of the Book

This book explores the often-overlooked relationship between college student activism and well-being. It features research from a multiphase study focused on bolstering student activist scholarship by sharing college student activists' perspectives on the relationship between their activism and their well-being. Core themes shared in this book follow and are mapped to individual chapters: (a) activism has yielded multiple benefits for student activists; (b) student activism is closely tied to students' identities; (c) non-negotiable costs of activism lead to burnout; and (d) students crave more university and community care. Through a combination of personal narratives, data analysis, and expert commentary, readers are offered a glimpse into the motivations that drive student activists in their pursuit of a more just and equitable society, the common challenges of burnout they face, and the strategies they employ to navigate these challenges and enhance their overall well-being.

Chapter 2 | Considering the Benefits of Being a Student Activist

College student activism is a noted component of high-impact learning practices (Kuh, 2008), critical to students' civic-minded leadership development, and central to a host of other positive student development outcomes (e.g., developing community, exploring personal values, committing to social change, building self-awareness) (Biddix, 2014; Harrison & Mather, 2017; Kezar et al., 2017; Martin et al., 2019). In a recent work, Pierce (2021) examined college student activists' sense of belonging in comparison to non-activist peers and, as a whole, found that activists reported more academic and intellectual development than non-activists, higher peer group interactions than non-activists, and more behaviors that led to integration at their institution than non-activists. Further, McCarron and colleagues (2024)—in their exploration of the relationship between SWB and activism—found that college student activists found joy from being in community with other student activists. These aforementioned benefits of activism to college student activists—in concert with the contributions of Biddix (2014), Biddix and colleagues (2009), Harrison and Mather (2017), Kezar and colleagues (2017), and Martin et al. (2019)—speak to aspects of well-being such as building relationships, finding purpose, growing sense of self and satisfaction, and focusing on holism (Diener, 2009; Ryff & Keyes, 1995; Seligman, 2011; Travis et al., 2020).

As such, this chapter attends to the nuances and contradictions related to activism from proper terminology to accurate descriptions of student motivations. It explores several domains, starting with civic engagement, where students may demonstrate learning and development gains from participation in on- and off-campus activism. The chapter then addresses how campuses benefit by supporting student activism, and concludes by discussing what campus educators can do to support students.

Chapter 3 | Who I Am Is What I Do: College Student Activists' Identities and Activism

Student resistance: A history of the unruly subject (Boren, 2019) extensively chronicled student movements in the U.S., tracing their origins from the early 20th century to contemporary manifestations within and beyond academic settings. Recent years have witnessed a notable upsurge in student activism, both domestically and internationally, fueled by ongoing historical inequities, systemic failures, and emerging issues (Baker & Blissett, 2018; Cole & Heinecke, 2020; Rhoads, 2009). Campus groups have utilized physical and digital platforms, such as social media (Eschmann, 2021), to amplify marginalized voices, making college student activism crucial in breaking the silence surrounding vulnerable communities (Kozuma, 2015).

To further this line of inquiry on college student activism, this chapter explores its driving forces, with a particular focus on the role of identity. Many interview participants cited identity as their primary motivation for engaging in activism. By delving into the complex interplay between activism and identity, this chapter provides valuable insights into the motivations and dynamics that drive student engagement in societal change.

Chapter 4 | Burnout: The Costs of Activism

Scholars have examined the experiences of activists hoping to create a "peaceful, sustainable, and life-affirming society" (Gomes, 1992, p. 138) and found that activists' emotional attachment to their work and their awareness of overwhelming social problems increased stress, self-inflicted pressure, isolation (Chen & Gorski, 2015), relationship burdens with other activists (Gomes, 1992), workload and time constraints (Vaccaro & Mena, 2011). Activists typically have unacknowledged and undervalued the emotional, mental, and physical risks of activism (Nair, 2004) leading to fatigue and "burnout" (Pines, 1994).

This risk of burnout and exhaustion can be painfully salient for college student activists. While all college students may experience some measure of stress (see American College Health Association [ACHA], 2018; Hartson et al., 2023), the effects on student activists may be much more robust given their negotiation of both the student and activist identity (e.g., Craddock, 2018). The interviewed college student activists reveal a prevalent experience of burnout, although their responses to burnout vary significantly. This chapter explores the causes, symptoms, and coping mechanisms employed by these student activists in response to burnout, shedding light on the multifaceted nature of burnout in college student activists.

Chapter 5 | Community: Bridging Self and Collective Care

This chapter addresses the personal, pedagogical, and institutional structures that empower and constrain student activist well-being. Rather than merely being supportive or constraining, each of these levels of community (student activist community, campus educators, and institutional structures) offers a complex mix of forces that can both hinder and empower student activist well-being.

By examining the interplay between campus, community, and student activism and adopting the SOFAR model that complicates relations between students (S), organization representatives (O), faculty (F), administrators (A), and residents (R) (Bringle et al., 2009), this chapter illuminates the multiplicity of roles these communities play in enhancing well-being and exacerbating stress. It underscores the importance of fostering supportive environments within colleges and universities, where student activists can find solace, encouragement, and a sense of belonging. Additionally, it emphasizes the need for institutions to address the challenges faced by student activists, acknowledging their contributions and providing the necessary support for their holistic well-being.

Chapter 6 | Reflection, Synthesis, and the Way Forward

Our research explored the experiences of 119 U.S. college student activists and examined how they attributed meaning to their activism and well-being. Through in-depth interviews, participants shared the personal costs and risks associated with their activism, as well as the factors that either mitigated or exacerbated their well-being. Notably, the significant costs related to time emerged as a prominent theme, alongside the dangers and risks of burnout. We also explored the intricate role of self-care, activist community, and the larger university environment, discovering that the meaning student activists ascribed to their activism was multifaceted, intertwined with both triumph and loss, and influenced by their intersecting identities.

In this conclusion, we discuss the research and practice implications of our findings across various disciplines, including social justice, human rights, leadership studies, and higher education. We offer policy recommendations and outline future directions that specifically address pressing issues such as mental health. By doing so, we aim to contribute to the ongoing discourse and inform actions that promote the well-being and effectiveness of student activists, while advancing positive social change.

References

Akhlaghpour, S., & Vaast, E. (2018). *Digital activism for social causes: Understanding clicktivism and substantive actions*. SSRN. https://doi.org/10.2139/ssrn.3220833

American College Health Association (ACHA). (2018). *National college health assessment II*. ACHA. www.acha.org/NCHA/ACHA-NCHA_Data/Publications_and_Reports/NCHA/Data/Reports_ACHA-NCHAIIc.aspx

Baker, D. J., & Blissett, R. S. L. (2018). Beyond the incident: Institutional predictors of student collective action. *Journal of Higher Education*, *89*(2), 184–207. https://doi.org/10.1080/00221546.2017.1368815

Biddix, J. P. (2014). Development through dissent: Campus activism as civic learning. *New Directions in Higher Education*, 2014(167), 73–85. https://doi.org/10.1002/he.20106

Biddix, J. P., Somers, P. A., & Polman, J. L. (2009). Protest reconsidered: Identifying democratic and civic engagement learning outcomes. *Innovation in Higher Education*, *34*(3), 133–147. https://doi.org/10.1007/s10755-009-9101-8

Boren, M. E. (2019). *Student resistance: A history of the unruly subject*. Routledge.

Bringle, R. G., Clayton, P. H., & Price, M. (2009). Partnerships in service learning and civic engagement. *Partnerships: A Journal of Service Learning & Civic Engagement*, *1*(1), 1–20. https://doi.org/10.7253/partj.v1i1.415

Cabrera, N. L. (2017). Activism or slacktivism? The potential and pitfalls of social media in contemporary student activism. *Journal of Diversity in Higher Education*, *10*(4), 400–415. https://doi.org/10.1037/dhe0000061

Charmaz, K. (2014). *Constructing grounded theory*. Sage.

Chen, C. W., & Gorski, P. C. (2015). Burnout in social justice and human rights activists: Symptoms, causes and implications. *Journal of Human Rights Practice*, *7*(3), 366–390. https://doi.org/10.1093/jhuman/huv011

Cole, R. M., & Heinecke, W. F. (2020). Higher education after neoliberalism: Student activism as a guiding light. *Policy Futures in Education*, *18*(1), 90–116. https://doi.org/10.1177/1478210318767459

Corbin, J., & Strauss, A. (2007). *Basics of qualitative research: Techniques and procedures for developing grounded theory* (3rd Ed.). Sage.

Couch, J. (2004). This is what democracy looks like : The genesis, culture and possibilities of anti-corporate activism. Unpublished PhD thesis, Victoria University, Melbourne.

Craddock, E. (2018). Doing "enough" of the "right" thing: The gendered dimension of the "ideal activist" identity and its negative emotional consequences. *Social Movement Studies*, *18*(2), 137–153. https://doi.org/10.1080/14742837.2018.6351555457

Creswell, J. W., & Creswell, J. D. (2018). *Research design: Qualitative, quantitative, and mixed methods approaches* (5th Ed.). Sage.

Creswell, J. W., & Poth, C. N. (2017). *Qualitative inquiry and research design: Choosing among five approaches* (4th Ed.). Sage.

Cudé, K. (2020). *Student activism across the past 5 years: What higher ed leaders need to know about evolving challenges.* EAB. https://eab.com/insights/infographic/student-affairs/student-activism-trends-2015-2020/

Diener, E. (2009). Subjective well-being. In E. Diener (Ed.), *The science of well-being: The collected works of Ed Diener* (pp. 11–58). Springer. https://doi.org/10.1007/978-90-481-2350-6_2

Diener, E., Scollon, C. N., & Lucas, R. E. (2009). The evolving concept of subjective well-being: The multifaceted nature of happiness. In E. Diener (Ed.), *Assessing well-being: The collected works of Ed Diener* (pp. 67–100). Springer. https://doi.org/10.1007/978-90-481-2354-4

Eschmann, R. (2021). Digital resistance: How online communication facilitates responses to racial microaggressions. *Sociology of Race and Ethnicity*, *7*(2), 264–277. https://doi.org/10.1177/2332649220933307

Glesne, C. (2016). *Becoming qualitative researchers: An introduction* (5th Ed.). Pearson.

Gomes, M. (1992). The rewards and stresses of social change: A qualitative study of peace activists. *Journal of Humanistic Psychology*, *32*(4), 138–146. https://doi.org/10.1177/0022167892324008

Harrison, L. M., & Mather, P. C. (2017). Making meaning of student activism: Student activist and administrator perspectives. *Mid-Western Educational Researcher*, *29*(2),117–135

Hartson, K. R., Hall, L. A., & Choate, S. A. (2023). Stressors and resilience are associated with well-being in young adult college students. *Journal of American College Health*, *71*(3), 821–829. https://doi.org/10.1080/07448481.2021.1908309

Jacoby, B. (2017). The new student activism: Supporting students as agents of social change. *Journal of College and Character*, *18*(1), 1–8. https://doi.org/10.1080/2194587x.2016.1260479

Jones, S. R., Torres, V., & Arminio, J. (2013). *Negotiating the complexities of qualitative research in higher education* (2nd Ed.). Routledge.

Keyes, C. L. M. (2006). Subjective well-being in mental health and human development research worldwide: An introduction. *Social Indices of Research*, *77*(1), 1–10. https://doi.org/10.1007/s11205-005-5550-3

Kezar, A., Acuña Avilez, A., Drivalas, Y., & Wheaton, M. M. (2017). Building social change oriented leadership capacity among student organizations: Developing students and campuses simultaneously. *New Directions in Student Leadership*, *155*, 45–57. https://doi.org/10.1002/yd.20249

Kozuma, H. (2015). *Student coalitions: Sites of development for student engagement and empowerment* (Publication No. 3704032) [Doctoral dissertation, University of Pennsylvania].

Kuh, G. D. (2008). *High-impact educational practices: What they are, who has access to them, and why they matter*. Association of American Colleges & Universities (AAC&U). www.aacu.org/publication/high-impact-educational-practices-what-they-are-who-has-access-to-them-and-why-they-matter

Linder, C., Quaye, S. J., Lange, A. C., Evans, M. E., & Stewart, T. J. (2019). *Identity-based student activism*. Routledge.

Maddux, J. E. (2018). Subjective well-being and life satisfaction: An introduction to conceptions, theories, and measures. In J. E. Maddux (Ed.), *Subjective well-being and life satisfaction* (pp. 3–26). Taylor and Francis.

Martin, G. L., Williams, B. M., Green, B., & Smith, M. J. (2019). Reframing activism as leadership. *New Directions in Student Leadership*, *161*, 9–24. https://doi.org/10.1002/yd.20317

McCarron, G. P., Chen, C. W., April, J., & LaMagdeleine, I. (2024). An exploratory study of the relationship between college student activists' labor and their subjective well-being: Perspectives from a U.S. institution. *Journal of American College Health.* 1–10. Online First. https://doi.org/10.1080/07448481.2024.2338409

Miller, M., & Nadler, D. (2018). College student activism on campus: Renewed interest or managed learning. In M. Miller & D. Tolliver (Eds.), *Exploring the technological, societal, and institutional dimensions of college student activism* (pp. 1–15). IGI Global.

Merriam, S. B., & Tisdell, E. J. (2016). *Qualitative research* (4th Ed.). Wiley.

Nair, N. (2004). On "being" and "becoming" … the many faces of an activist. *Agenda*, *18*(60), 28–32. https://doi.org/10.1080/10130950.2004.9674533

Pierce, J. E. (2021). *Belonging through dissent: A national study of student activist sense of belonging and institutional integration.* (Publication No. 28411444) [Doctoral dissertation, University of Georgia].

Pines, A. M. (1994). Burnout in political activism: An existential perspective. *Journal of Health and Human Resources Administration*, *16*(4), 381–394.

Rhoads, R. A. (2009). Learning from students as agents of social change: Toward an emancipatory vision of the university. *Journal of Change Management*, *9*(3), 309–322. https://doi.org/10.1080/14697010903125555

Ryff, C. D., & Keyes, C. L. M. (1995). The structure of psychological well-being revisited. *Journal of Personality and Social Psychology*, *69*(4), 719–727. https://doi.org/10.1037/0022-3514.69.4.719

Seligman, M. E. P. (2011). *Flourish: A visionary new understanding of happiness and well-being*. Simon & Schuster.

Sims, D., & Cilliers, F. (2023). Qualitatively speaking: Deciding how much data and analysis is enough. *African Journal of Health Professions Education*, *15*(1), 2–3. https://doi.org/10.7196/AJHPE.2023.v15i1.1657

Travis, J., Kaszycki, A., Geden, M., & Bunde, J. (2020). Some stress is good stress: The challenge-hindrance framework, academic self-efficacy, and academic outcomes. *Journal of Educational Psychology*, *112*(8), 1632–1643. https://doi.org/10.1037/edu0000478

Vaccaro, A., & Mena, J. (2011). It's not burnout, it's more: Queer college activists of color and mental health. *Journal of Gay and Lesbian Mental Health*, *15*(4), 339–367. https://doi.org/10.1080/19359705.2011.600656

2 Considering the Benefits of Being a Student Activist

> *I started like learning that the Latin culture is not only about my culture that is a Bolivian culture, but it's big and that there is always something to relate to. And for those things that you know you can relate to, you find a family, you find friends, you bond with people, which is beautiful. So that bond—that family—pushed me to look for positions in the exec board and to fight more for the awareness and for the diversity on campus.*—Violet

In the passage above, participant Violet discussed how she changed as a result of friends encouraging her to join the Latino Student Alliance in college.

Introduction

In May 2024, the cover of a *New Yorker* magazine depicted a farcical illustration of a college student adorned in graduation garb receiving their diploma from a faculty member. However, upon closer inspection, the viewer could see that the student was among several whose hands were bound in handcuffs for presumably participating in the prominent and controversial spring 2024 campus protests. The cover was intended to be a comedic commentary on the fate of student activists responding to the overflowing tensions on many campuses following Hamas' attack on Israel on October 7, 2023, and Israel's war in Gaza. The conflict reached new levels when pro-Palestinian protestors erected encampments on campuses across the United States, and counterprotests targeted these visible demonstrations. Students who supported the pro-Palestinian efforts were threatened by some

DOI: 10.4324/9781003481010-2

campuses with sanctions and even a delay in the issuing of diplomas (Haidar & Kettles, 2024).

In an environment where one-third of surveyed students who participated in pro-Palestinian protests claimed that job offers had been retracted after they revealed their participation (Alonso, 2024), it may not be clear how students benefit from participating in activism. However, even in the same survey of student protestors (Alonso, 2024), more than half of the respondents claimed that involvement in activism actually improved their prospects of finding a job after graduation.

Describing student activism in terms of benefits can be thorny. Although students can benefit in a host of ways as described below, when they get involved in activist efforts (Schwartz et al., 2023), the term "benefit" does not adequately describe the caveats and complexities students may face when participating in activism. This chapter begins by attending to the nuances and contradictions related to activism, from proper terminology to accurate descriptions of student motivations. We explore several domains, starting with civic engagement, where students may demonstrate learning and development gains from participation in on- and off-campus activism. We then address how campuses benefit by supporting student activism, and the chapter concludes by addressing what campus educators can do to support students.

Literature Review

The Contested Nature of "Benefits"

As discussed in Chapter One, students engage in a variety of behaviors seeking fairness and justice that are often called activism but may also be labeled as resistance, organizing, mobilizing, and awareness-raising (Linder et al., 2019). These actions are also forms of civic engagement, but not all forms of civic engagement would be considered activism. Whereas civic engagement is defined as "individual and collective actions designed to identify and address issues of public concern" (American Psychological Association [APA], 2024, para. 2), activism specifically addresses injustice affecting a group or community, and engaging in activism is intended to bring about or prevent a change (Hemer & Reason, 2021).

Activism Defined

Activism contains three dimensions: Focusing on an issue identified as a public good, addressing an injustice toward a group or population, and bringing about change (Hemer & Reason, 2021). A variety of behaviors has been identified as activism including community organizing, advocacy work, protesting and demonstrations, direct service, and formal political activities (Iowa and Minnesota Campus Compact, n.d.).

The terminology is important because it signifies the motivations of the student and their socio-political reality. This terminology is not just a discussion of preferred semantics, it also influences how the notion of benefits for student activists is understood.

For example, a student of color at a predominantly White institution (PWI) may find that the term resistance is a more apt description for their behavior rather than activism. It is not unusual for minoritized students at a PWI to find that when they seek to take advantage of services such as leadership opportunities, student support programs, and prominent scholarships supposedly available to them they face microaggressions and doubts. Availing themselves of these programs then may not feel like activism even if unbeknownst to them, their actions of resistance are aligned with the definition of activism.

Activism is the Priority

Simply seeking to express one's social identity fully and authentically could lead to mistreatment. How one speaks, dresses, comports oneself, and shares aspects of their identity could put a minoritized student at risk for mistreatment. In a campus milieu that tends toward unfairness, publicly identifying with one's minoritized identity could be seen as an act of resistance. For example, on a campus with overt heterosexist policies and behaviors, when an educator or administrator suggests that a student who openly identifies as Queer accrues benefits from being out, we ignore the true social reality for the student (Linder et al., 2020). Even if the student does achieve some benefit from living more authentically, reducing this experience to the "benefits of being out" while disregarding the risks is potentially troubling. Framing the student's experience only through the lens of benefits shifts the perspective from the students to the educator. That is, discounting the complexity and challenges of persisting in a heterosexist environment to focus solely on how the student may gain some advantage by not being closeted, allows the administrator to rationalize troubling aspects of the campus environment. Chapter Three of this volume explores this issue in more depth by examining how issues of identity and intersectionality shape student activist well-being.

Commonly, students who do not identify as activists may engage in behaviors that could be considered activism (Linder et al., 2019; Shenberger, 2022). Making demands for more inclusive academic offerings, organizing for campus programming, and petitioning for changes in campus policies are forms of student activism. To students, though, these efforts are part of their passion and perhaps an aspect of their involvement in a student organization, but the behaviors are synonymous with activism. Other students may engage in advocacy work through a campus or non-profit organization that raises awareness about societal inequity, unfairness, and oppression on- or off-campus and again, while this is activism, a student may apply a different label such as awareness-raising.

As we describe below, there are unambiguous benefits that students glean from these behaviors, but attaining the benefits is typically not the primary motivation for the student. This distinction is important because when administrators, faculty, and staff with a benefits mindset interact with equity-minded students, activists may feel misunderstood and frustrated, reinforcing mistrust and exposing administrator naivete.

While students derive skills, attitudes, relationships, community, meaning, and identity from being involved in activism (Chittum et al., 2022; Linder et al., 2019; Martin et al., 2019; McCarron et al., 2024; Pierce, 2021), when faculty and staff frame the involvement in terms of benefits it can seem patronizing and appear to students as a fundamental misunderstanding of their motivations for community work (Harrison & Mather, 2017; Linder et al., 2020). Student activists may seek an administrator who understands their concerns. When we describe it solely in developmental terms without acknowledging the thrust of student demands, we are inadvertently announcing to students that "we don't get it." Central to student activist organizing is the inherent unfairness in systems, which runs contrary to administrators who are charged with upholding those same systems (Harrison & Mather, 2017). This can lead to misunderstanding and mutual frustration. We assert that administrators need to possess a nuanced understanding of how students benefit from participation in activism so we can bolster environments that facilitate student learning and development. Simultaneously, we also must be mindful of the differences in power and perspective that exist between students and educators to effectively build trust (Linder et al., 2020; McCarron et al., 2024).

Students have the power to illuminate the misalignment between the stated objectives of higher education and current practices (Hoffman & Mitchell, 2016). Activism then can lead to uncomfortable truths and potential defensiveness amongst administrators (Harrison & Mather, 2017). Jacoby (2017) reminds educators that our job is to support students in understanding the range of activism tools at their disposal as well as the implications of using them. Ultimately those conversations are not only preparing students with the knowledge and skills to work toward social change, but for being more effective members of a democracy. The power of student activism is that it can facilitate gains in civic engagement (Chittum et al., 2022). This next section provides an overview of those civic engagement elements as well as the role that engaging in activism plays in supporting that development.

Activism as a Form of Civic Engagement

Hemer and Reason (2021) joined other scholars who place student activism within the larger body of civic engagement literature. Civic engagement encompasses a variety of competencies, skills, and attitudes. Activism and political action as a form of civic engagement is well supported in the literature. This section outlines that literature as well as the beneficial outcomes of developing civic engagement skills, attitudes, and behaviors. It also addresses the difficulty of doing that within the current contentious context. When students engage civically they are not only making strides toward important education outcomes such as personal and social responsibility, persistence, openness to difference, improved grades, and collaboration skills (Chittum et al., 2022), but also civic engagement in and of itself is an essential outcome for developing the skills and attitudes for being a member of a democracy (Welch & Saltmarsh, 2016).

Civic Mindedness

Steinberg and colleagues (2011), for example, proposed a civic-minded graduate model suggesting a form of civic engagement that could serve as a goal for an undergraduate education. Civic-minded graduates would develop a civic identity, which is defined as the sense of responsibility a student feels when joining with others to work "towards public purposes" (American Association of Colleges & Universities [AAC&U], n.d., p. 1).

Civic-minded graduates would develop an appreciation that the learning they have gained in college or university is not only for furthering their own goals, but also to enhance the public good (Steinberg et al., 2011). Lastly, civic mindedness suggests that graduates integrate community involvement, including political action into their lives beyond college. The community involvement identified in this model implies that a student may be inspired to be involved in that action from a burgeoning sense of community responsibility and a desire to use one's education to foster public goals. Conversely, it is also likely that a student may discover a passion for a particular social concern or may feel the need to speak out on a pressing matter, which contributes to strengthening one's civic identity (Steinberg et al., 2011).

High-Impact Practices

Pedagogies and programs associated with deeper learning and positive outcomes of persistence, critical thinking, and openness to diversity have been termed High-Impact Practices (HIPs; Kuh, 2008). Practices include a range of interventions from undergraduate research to first-year experience programming. However civic and community engagement was highlighted in a recent research synthesis for its unique contribution to student learning (Chittum et al., 2022). Specifically, service learning, the practice of integrating curriculum with community concerns, was associated with most developmental gains in a variety of domains. The synthesis also uncovered meaningful relationships between other, more general community-based engagement experiences and outcomes such as "increases in civic attitudes and civic mindedness … and feeling civic and social responsibility or obligation" (Chittum et al., 2022, p. 16). Since the introduction of the notion of HIPs, concerns have persisted about the access that minoritized students have to these practices (Chittum et al., 2022; Kuh, 2008). Furthermore, when minoritized students do participate in HIPs questions remain about whether the practices are consistently high-impact (Chittum et al., 2022; Kuh, 2008).

Activism as a Less Visible Form of Civic Engagement

As explained, civic and community engagement have evolved to encompass a wide and diverse range of practices. It is common for individual campuses to tout their voter engagement and service learning offerings. Some may go further to promote community-based research and social change efforts at local, national, and global levels (Chittum et al., 2022; Steinberg et al., 2011; Welch & Saltmarsh, 2016). In contrast, student activism is often not promoted by campus civic and community engagement departments. Not surprisingly, campuses are not universally welcoming of protests and demonstrations, particularly ones on their campuses (Linder et al., 2019; Martin et al., 2019). While campuses endorse outcomes like "civic mindedness, social responsibility, political engagement, and social change" (Martin et al., 2019, p. 9), they may be considerably less likely to advocate for the behaviors and actions—the rallies, occupations, marches, and other forms of protest—that lead to these outcomes. Even though administrators may be reluctant to encourage student activism, scholars have asserted that participation in activism is indeed civic engagement (Biddix, 2014; Keeling & Associates, 2004).

Activism as Civic Action

Jacoby (2017) proposed that contemporary manifestations of student activism differ from previous forms of student protest because of the focus on holding institutions of higher education accountable for their potential involvement or complicity in national and international concerns. These definitions counter the reactive understanding that student dissent is simply disruptive and problematic. Hemer and Reason (2021) summarized activism as a "multidimensional construct representing many different practices of dissent" (p. 37). Student activism addresses a wide array of on- and off-campus concerns including "war; corporate takeovers; the persistence of poverty, violence, and bigotry; and policies and practices that contribute to continued environmental degradation. In addition, student activists fight to make higher education accessible to a greater number of minoritized populations" (Hoffman & Mitchell, 2016, p. 278).

Activism Promotes Complex Reasoning

Kornbluh and colleagues (2022) differentiated between civic behaviors that seek to reform or correct current political alignments and structures with those that critique and challenge these same structures. The former works to make change in alignment with the current political arrangement, while the latter uses more activist approaches to illuminate systems and challenge them. Based on previous research and other studies (e.g., Linder et al., 2019; Morgan et al., 2021), Kornbluh and collaborators posited that students would develop civic beliefs by finding their way into activism through a personal connection to a particular social concern. This can eventually lead to a student's appreciation for how one specific social concern intersects with other related issues.

Freire's (1970/1986) notion of critical consciousness provides a meaningful framework to conceptualize a relationship between civic behaviors and civic beliefs leading to activism. The three components are: (1) critical reflection (i.e., connecting individual injustices to larger systems); (2) critical motivation (i.e., believing in one's efficacy in collaborating with others); and (3) critical action (i.e., behaviors intended to effectively bring about change).

The skill of reflection where one can simultaneously analyze a situation at the individual and societal level, the understanding of how to effectively collaborate with those that are different from oneself, and the experience of bringing about change are powerful knowledge, skill, and self-awareness outcomes that are intertwined with the goals of higher education (Owen, 2016). Student activism then contains the potential for students to develop these complex reasoning skills (Baxter Magolda & King, 2012).

Activism Outcomes Are 21st-Century Skills

Despite the constant drumbeat sounded by critics that higher education only indoctrinates students in leftist, progressive attitudes and does not effectively prepare graduates for jobs (Dickey, 2024), the annual survey of employers by the AAC&U (Finley, 2023) dispels these myths. Over 1000 executives and hiring managers were interviewed and more than 80% agreed that college prepares graduates to be successful in the workforce. Furthermore, these employers endorsed a well-rounded, liberal-arts education that promotes critical and complex thinking including involvement in community-based experiences (Finley, 2023). While activism itself was not addressed in the report, skills employed by student activists overlap with the requisite skills for a 21st-century workforce (Finley, 2023).

This overview describes how student efforts to interrupt or instigate change and turn back injustices in the service of the public good (Hemer & Reason, 2021) is an element of high-impact educational practices that can lead to civic skills, attitudinal shifts, and behaviors. Furthermore, the complexity of thought involved in civic action contributes to a form of civic mindedness and 21st-century skills. The chapter began with a quote from Violet, one of our participants, describing the experience of finding a community as she sought to build an awareness of campus diversity. The next section brings forward more participant voices to explore how our participants reflect and trouble the extant literature.

Findings

In this section we highlight findings from the study described in Chapter One of this volume with themes and quotes from participants. The focus here is on how participants interpreted the notion of benefits from activism and the ways that their participation in activist behaviors had beneficial effects.

Interpreting the Notion of Benefits

Participants in the study described mixed feelings with the idea of benefits from participating in activism. Aaliyah, a Black woman seeking racial justice and health equity, summed up these thoughts: "Like it's a lot of mixed feelings that comes with the word activism." Those competing feelings emerged from an appreciation that being labeled an activist evoked the inspiring influence that students can have on their peers. However, Aaliyah lamented that students needed to even work to address issues that in her mind should have been settled: "The fact that we have to do this in the first place, like be working towards some of the most basic human rights. Like that sometimes gets to me."

Axel, a non-binary identifying student focused on racial justice, sought to clarify that while they may develop skills as a result of serving as activists and organizers, this is not their motivation:

> I really don't think of that as an opportunity to develop leadership skills. I really just see it as an opportunity to do something that I believe in. And, you know, if I discover new skills while doing it, that's great, but that's not something that I would really consider a priority.

Chrissy, a White woman working on graduate and professional student rights, sought to put her efforts in clear terms: "I would not probably use the term activist to describe myself, just because I've just tried to do the right thing. And that's the bare minimum." Violet likened her activist efforts to parenting. Violet noted that parents do not seek a tangible product in return for their instinctive care of their children. Similarly, Violet described that the priority of her efforts was solely directed at the growth of the members of her Latinx organization: "So I do it without interest without trying to receive something in exchange."

Study participants described benefitting from activism such as building meaningful relationships, developing leadership skills, increasing self-awareness, and discovering a more robust sense of purpose, but spoke of these benefits as ancillary to their reason for engaging in these efforts. Aaliyah's experience of conflicted feelings regarding benefits captures the essence of many of our participants. Aaliyah appreciated the ways she gained from her involvement. However, when activists were seeking to restore what she described as essential human rights, the idea of benefitting from such a struggle was troubling and far from a priority. This finding supports previous literature suggesting that focusing on benefits to student activists while discounting the content or focus of the activism will fundamentally misunderstand the mindset and motivation of student activists.

Activism as a Form of Participant Civic Engagement

In describing their experience with student activism, study participants demonstrated civic mindedness, engagement in high-impact practices, taking civic action, using complex reasoning, and employing 21st-century skills.

Student Perceptions of Civic Mindedness

Understanding that one's education goes beyond personal benefit to include responsibility to enhance the public good is an indicator of civic mindedness (Steinberg et al., 2011). When describing their experience with student activism participants seemed to unintentionally describe their civic-minded orientation. For example, Aaliyah, like other participants, described her college experience as containing a challenging amount of stress, particularly during pandemic lockdowns. Aaliyah was taking on highly demanding activist roles and despite the stress of the responsibility, she also felt "fulfilled when I knew I was in service to other people." Aaliyah acknowledged that she suffered because she had not prioritized self-care and only derived fulfillment from her activism. When Aaliyah worked on re-prioritizing her mental health, she did not discount her commitment to activism and sense of responsibility.

Chloe, a Latina student seeking to address food insecurity, described metaphorically wearing "three or four hats" and managing the stress of multiple demands from being a student to doing an internship to being involved on campus: "But then you just have to remember like why you're doing it in the first place. And that makes it a little bit easier." While this still could lead a student to experience burnout, as explored in Chapter Four, Chloe also addresses the sense of responsibility students feel as a member of the student body. Chrissy echoed these sentiments describing long hours of advocacy work intertwined with her academic work. Each activity bolstering the other.

Amanda, a Latina student trying to reduce sexual violence and address rights for women, when elaborating on the terms activism and leadership described a deep inner sense of justice and a need to act: "there's been a wrong and that wrong needs to be righted." She acknowledged the complexity in seeking redress and therefore openness and learning are crucial in her drive to achieve justice. Cameron, an Asian woman attempting to expand cultural awareness, portrayed how she structured her class schedule to allow for her to practice her advocacy work. Cameron works to debunk cultural stereotypes during the evenings when she knows many of her classmates will be accessible. Cameron defined the way she took leadership as actions that serve a larger public good: "It's taking ownership and taking the initiative to not only help yourself but to help other people and guide them." Jason, an Asian man working for environmental justice, shared how he uses his courses to pursue his activism: "I bring that into my school and for my family. So when I'm like writing a marketing paper, it's usually about environmental topics. So whenever like a writing project, I talked about fast fashion, or climate change."

These participants are articulating the responsibility that comes with pursuing a formal education. Their activism was influenced by their education and the activism influenced their learning.

Student Experiences with High-Impact Practices

In Kuh's (2008) description of the essential elements of high-impact practices he outlines the importance of student in-depth involvement in purposeful activity, consistent student interaction with peers and faculty about consequential topics, dialogue with individuals who are different from themselves, and the opportunity for frequent feedback about one's performance. Participants in the study often described elements of their activism that reflected many of these key high-impact ingredients.

Christina, a Black woman pursuing education equity and increased transparency, served in a mentorship program supporting local minoritized students. This provided her the opportunity to offer the kind of role modeling that she did not receive at that age. This kind of initiative allowed Christina to be involved in a purposeful program and consistent interaction with other peer mentors who possessed a different racial identity. This differed from another campus organizational experience where Christina was feeling disillusioned after losing their advisor and their action being redundant.

Alexis, a Latina student, also spoke of working with peers on meaningful projects related to criminal justice reform:

> You also get to know what type of individual they are and what they're passionate about … might align with your own and that that's a way you can … really work alongside them for whatever project you might have in the future.

Alexis acknowledged she hoped to become better at holding conversations with students from different backgrounds and recalled misgivings about past conversations where she would share in-depth about herself: "without asking questions about the other person even more so kind of going deeper into what they think. I just think those types of conversations I still need my practicing."

Violet offered the metaphor of ants to describe how she saw her activism:

> They can carry three times their own weight, which is amazing. And if you think about it, we are all like little ants when it comes to activism. We're all doing something to make for a better community. Right? … We're working as a team. We're trying to make our community better.

This metaphor speaks to the importance of working across differences on shared and purposeful commitments.

Axel, who had been contributing to grassroots organizing to change the names of campus buildings described why she referred to her work as organizing as opposed to activism:

> Activism and organizing, I mean, they are very similar terms … When I think of an activist, I think of, you know, an individual person with a megaphone and a protest sign, you know, leading chants or whatever. When I think of organizing, I think of it as much more community-based and … groups of like-minded people coming together, and developing clear demands for what they need.

Axel elaborated that their work was on behalf of the student body who communicated their opposition to buildings being named after individuals who did not reflect their values.

These narratives reflect high-impact practices in action. Participating in activism immerses students in meaningful work, working on consequential concerns with peers and faculty, engaging in dialogue across differences, and receiving feedback on the effects of one's efforts.

Student Perceptions of Participation in Civic Engagement

Study participants spoke of the importance of being acknowledged for the contributions of their activism. Some participants, like Chloe, sought more support for their activism by having administration "hear" students. They described how profound it would be for administration to listen to their concerns. Violet noted how deflating it is that her organization initiates significant community building and advocacy but felt that "the university never says anything." Students were seeking recognition both for the additional labor of being an activist and specifically for the content of their concerns. Chrissy relayed how university administrators were dismissive of her work on a controversial campaign: “It was really disheartening to hear like a roomful of people making six figures … Just kind of saying, look, the social justice issues are not important.” Chrissy’s feeling reflects the ambivalence of administrators toward activists highlighted in the literature. While colleges and universities will profile civic and community engagement efforts, the experiences of study participants demonstrate the reluctance that university administrations may have about spotlighting and, as Linder and colleagues (2019) implore, “embracing” student activists. Jacob, a Jewish White man working on bringing about racial and environmental justice, provided a nuanced critique of his institution’s strong service ethic. Jacob found that in one respect the university’s service slogan was used to mask less flattering aspects of the institution, yet that same slogan does seem to simultaneously channel a more activist mindset.

Student Experience with Civic Action

From advocating for peers who are food insecure and addressing the campus racial climate to working against sexual violence and organizing for criminal justice reform, participants were engaged in a wide range of concerns. Regardless of the issue, participants were unhesitating about their commitment to activism. Abigail, a White woman working on reducing sexual violence and improving women’s rights, mentioned the importance of: “standing up for what you believe in.” Chrissy said: “I never get tired, I guess, of advocating for people.” Abigail described the power of affecting not just regional and national change, but global transformation: “I would feel hopeful that our generation is doing something to help.”

Students’ Complex Reasoning

Participants recounted how their thinking expanded as they reflected on their engagement. As the examples below demonstrate, some participants clearly had been engaging in a process of critical reflection where they were making linkages between their individual experience and larger social issues, engaging with a diverse group of students and community members, and pondering their efficacy for bringing about change. In addition, participants found the interview process itself to be an intervention to promote reflection.

Chloe discussed how she appreciated building relationships with students who used the services of the campus food pantry. As she pondered the experience of these students, she began to think of the larger system of food insecurity leading her to consider advocacy. At that point, Chloe's perspective on her work with the pantry shifted from seeking an experience to pursuing a passion for impacting the larger social concern. Similarly, Bob, a White man focused on education, described how getting involved as a student staff person in the Community Engagement office led him to facilitate service projects and reflection activities. Bob reflected how leading others led him to be more thoughtful: "Gives me the opportunity to check my biases and keep learning. This, in turn, allows me to lead others more effectively." Haley described how getting involved despite some apprehension as a White person in Black Lives Matter protests while also taking leadership in an organization that supports children with cancer, challenged her to better understand the larger issues associated with these causes. She also noted how her thinking changed when things progressed from knowledge to action.

Kelsey discussed the meaning she was making from her involvement in climate change and anti-racism causes. She explored how her class privilege and the racism she experiences due to her Asian identity affected her when she participated in climate change demonstrations in Washington, DC. Kelsey described her reflections on being Asian in the primarily White environmental movement and while also seeing attendees at rallies who seemed more focused on self-promotion, which provided her with new insight into her motivation and role. Kelsey was continuing to reflect on what it meant to be a spokesperson and to consider herself knowledgeable enough to speak out on a particular issue.

Laura G., focused on advocacy for the Global South, appreciated the opportunity to participate in activist efforts. Laura G. noticed how being both South Asian and entering college identifying as "shy" was challenging when activism required speaking out in ways that initially felt unpracticed and uncomfortable. As Laura G.'s confidence slowly grew and their activist identity expanded, Laura G. faced a new obstacle when their non-partisan organization was prevented from taking political action. This led to insights about their role and expectations for making an impact.

Student Perceptions of Skill Development

Participants described a wide variety of leadership skills that developed as a result of their activism. While numerous participants were quick to point out that their motivation was not to establish skills, they nonetheless were engaged in developing a host of formal leadership competencies such as: Managing an executive board, facilitating meetings, event planning, complex and strategic communication with various constituencies, volunteer management and support, public speaking, establishing trusted dialogues with university leadership, and networking.

Students often developed skills as they needed to practice them. For instance, Anna R., a South Asian woman seeking to reduce food insecurity, and Haley, a White woman supporting children with terminal illnesses, took on formal organizational leadership roles before they intended to, but when the organization required them. Both students described the challenge as a learning process of taking on leadership before they thought they were ready.

Benjamin, identifying as non-binary and White working on LGBTQ+ rights and politics and policy, described how different it is to pursue meaningful system change compared with other activities like sports:

> So when you're a leader in sports and you want to lead a team to success you know there's things that you can do to impact immediate change. But there [activism] you can't really do that … So I think learning patience as a leader was super important.

Kyle, a Black man who uses art in social media to advocate for anti-racism and anti-sexism, described the importance of being: "bold enough to take the first step and do things that are seen as outside norms."

Veronica, a South Asian woman supporting individuals with mental health concerns, expressed the importance of not defining leadership as a command-and-control role, but one that is about "empowering" other members of your team to be successful. Alexis and Amanda expressed similar sentiments. When describing an ideal leader, Axel provided an effective summary of the kinds of leadership skills participants were learning:

> The things that make them such good leaders is that they don't see themselves as the center of attention. They … don't see themselves

> as leaders. They kind of see themselves as followers, and that they're following the needs and the wants of the people who they're advocating for which in sort of a roundabout way, makes them a really good leader for the groups that they're advocating for.

Discussion and Implications for Research and Practice

Recent qualitative studies have described how students engaged in activism have developed leadership skills such as organizing, critical thinking, effective communication, and working across differences (Kezar et al., 2017; Linder et al., 2020; Martin et al., 2019; Owen et al., 2022). In addition to skill development, engaging in activism provides students with an opportunity to view and critique the performance of leadership. Kezar and colleagues (2017) and Owen and collaborators (2022) noted earlier studies where students engaged in activism challenged traditional command-and-control approaches to leadership and embraced a less hierarchical and power-based approach.

Participants in this study reflected the findings from previous scholarship. They described developing similar skills to those listed above. However, participants also unequivocally stated that if they were the beneficiary of skill development from their activism that was not their primary or even secondary motivation for engaging in these behaviors. Instead, participants typically described their skills humbly and as an afterthought.

The terminology that participants used to describe their activism also helps us understand how they conceive their roles, their motivations, and their positionality. Students often referred to their efforts as organizing, education, and service, and were reluctant with the term "activist" being applied to them. Participants respected activists, but their perception of activists was often divorced from how they saw themselves. From the perspective of participants, activists took bold action often singularly. They often described working collaboratively and not seeking the limelight. Several participants mentioned Greta Thunberg, the Swedish youth climate change activist, as a high-profile example. Like so many well-known activists preceding them, Thunberg is often mis-characterized as acting individually without any indication of the necessary preparation, planning, collaborating, and organizing that their work requires. When students described their own behaviors, they were keenly aware of the detail-oriented work with their peers and the need to be knowledgeable and abreast of the latest updates necessary to proudly stand for whatever the issue may be.

It is common for students of color, trans, and gender nonconforming students to engage in activism not because they choose to be an activist, but because they feel obligated to carve out spaces where they might flourish (Linder et al., 2020; Nicolazzo, 2016). Students like Violet, whose quote began this chapter, and other participants reflect this description.

Although participants typically did not use the label of activist to describe their activist behaviors, their actions often aligned with the definition of activism: They almost always were focused on a public good like supporting recently arrived immigrants and refugees, reducing injustice in the prison system, promoting climate justice, and anti-racism. These efforts were intended to restore justice to a group or community. Plus, the students were change oriented—with many working tirelessly—often at a cost to their mental health.

When students hold campuses, communities, corporations, and other entities accountable to stated values and ethical standards they are demonstrating the civic engagement skills that most colleges and universities seek for graduates. These actions are also illustrative of a care and concern for those entities. At first blush, a demonstration, rally, protest, or other kind of public action, may be experienced by administrators as embarrassing, misdirected, naïve, rash, or illegal. However, as profiled above, students are also showcasing Freire's critical pedagogy notion of praxis (Kornbluh et al., 2022; Owen, 2016). That is, students are seeking to connect theory to practice, which is precisely what higher education is intended to prize. Students' efforts may not always be polished, they may bypass what seem to administrators as essential steps, the effort may be a work in progress, or a specific campus rule or guideline may be violated. Yet, when administrators respond solely from these frustrations, educators are missing out on facilitating learning, enhancing student mattering, and bolstering student relationships with administration (Linder et al., 2016; Owen et al., 2022). Linder (2019) proposed an alternative: "embracing these students as leaders may result in better relationships between student activists and educational administrators and improved educational climates for minoritized students" (p. 90).

Despite pressures on administrators from critics to silence protestors, both entities—students and institutions of higher education—benefit from student activism. Students develop a broad range of civic engagement skills, they enhance their awareness of their social identity, their subjective well-being has the potential to improve, and they build community leading to persistence. Colleges and universities benefit, as well. While most campus senior-level administrators are not eager to have prolonged demonstrations, these student-led efforts on- and off-campus contribute to students developing the above outcomes that most campuses seek. When students advocate for equity, inclusion, and fairness on their campus they are demonstrating care, but they are also helping their institution improve. There are countless examples where student protest demands eventually led to new programs, initiatives, and commitments that would make colleges and universities more welcoming.

Conclusion

Student activism is a unique form of student involvement. Elements of the curriculum and co-curriculum such as critical thinking, systems-thinking, effective communication, planning, and applying theory to practice (Conner, 2023; Farago et al., 2018; Kezar et al., 2017; Kornbluh et al., 2022; Linder et al., 2020; Martin et al., 2019; Owen et al., 2022) are essential parts of student activism. The civic engagement skills and knowledge required to organize, raise awareness, and advocate prepare graduates to be effective democratic citizens. These elements of critical consciousness, dialogue, and praxis proposed by Freire (1970/1986) are complex cognitive processes that involve taking leadership, building community, and engaging civically (Kezar et al., 2017; Linder et al., 2020; Martin et al., 2019; Owen et al., 2022). Even when minoritized students are engaging in these efforts to create a student community where none exists, they create a sense of belonging (Linder et al., 2020; Nicolazzo, 2016; Warnock & Hurst, 2016). Most forms of student activism seek to increase awareness and address societal inequalities and unfairness (Farago et al., 2018; Hoffman & Mitchell, 2016).

When the news spread in the spring of 2024 of student encampments and counterprotests including violent student behaviors, and student arrests, it would be easy to lose sight of the positive impact of the activism. Participating in a form of activism prepares students for a world overflowing with uncertainty (Jay, 2024). When students use their education to join with others to address injustice and seek to change policy, shift the way we think, and choose to act, they are fulfilling the goals of a college education. Student activists demonstrate efficacy and they debunk the myth of "snowflakes." Engaging with difference, dialoguing with officials with different levels of access to power, and taking a public stand are essential 21st-century skills. Our role as educators is to understand the diversity of our students and support them as they find their motivation for aligning values and action. Educators can work with students in making connections to the ideas and theories embedded in the curriculum and support reflection on the characteristics of being an involved member of a democracy. We can work to expand student self-awareness, assist students in considering their goals, and help them think through the potential ramifications of their choices. In our capacity, we facilitate student learning and development, and student activism is a powerful vehicle in which to accomplish those goals.

Scholarship in Action
Considering the Benefits of Being a Student Activist

Thought Questions:

For students: There are a variety of forms of student activism and regardless of the type they hold the potential to build a student's sense of belonging and a feeling like they matter. What is a student activism opportunity you could pursue that could enhance your sense of community?

For staff/practitioners: During campus protests it is common for student activists and administrators to both report feeling misunderstood and disappointed by the other entity. Harrison and Mather (2017), Kornbluh and colleagues (2022), and Stewart and collaborators (2020) describe how student activism addresses unjust and inequitable systems, which can inspire defensiveness from administrators. How can you work with colleagues to enhance understanding of student activist motivations and goals?

For faculty: Scholars such as Harrison and Mather (2017), Linder and colleagues (2019), Hoffman and Mitchell (2016), Jacoby (2017), and Kezar and colleagues (2017) describe roles educators can play in supporting student learning, development, and well-being. What is an action you can take that is direct, indirect, and/or through advocacy that facilitates critical reflection and consciousness?

For community partners: Researchers have described how student activists employ systems-thinking when they make connections between injustice and potential actions to address that injustice. How can you help students reflect on the role that injustice plays in the community and one actionable way to address that injustice?

For researchers: Flett (2022) described the importance of expanding research on student mattering (as opposed to marginalization) and McCarron and colleagues (2023) pursued this through their research on the mattering of student activists. This area is ripe for additional scholarship. What are research questions you can pose that would explore how campuses can create more mattering environments for student activists?

Resources for Additional Learning:

Websites:

Student activists are at risk for feelings of burnout because they are typically balancing a full-time course load, possibly a job, and the strenuous demands of activism and involvement. In addition, activism can lead to feelings of frustration and disappointment. This WebMd website provides an overview of the symptoms of burnout and strategies for addressing these challenging, albeit normal feelings.

https://www.webmd.com/mental-health/burnout-symptoms-signs

Books:

Jay, M. (2024). *The twentysomething treatment.* Simon & Schuster

Dr. Meg Jay's book describes the unique challenges of the decade when students and recent alums are in their 20s. This is a time of extreme uncertainty and these unknowns in a world replete with unique global stressors, make this an exceptionally challenging time. Jay provides evidence-based strategies for Twentysomethings to address the unknowns and the attendant stress.

Gervais, M. (2023). *The first rule of mastery: Stop worrying about what people think of you.* Harvard Business Review Press.

This book is fitting for student activists who typically have to navigate tensions between peer, family, faculty, and administrator expectations. Gervais guides readers to understand their values-based purpose to more effectively communicate authentically and acknowledge areas for learning and growth.

Cann, C. & DeMeulenaere, E. (2020). *The activist academic: Engaged scholarship for resistance, hope and social change.* Myers Education Press.

This volume provides inspiration for scholars through narratives, strategies, and resources to explore how to connect personal commitments with scholarship.

Classroom Activities:

It is common in Community-Based Learning reflection environments to use the story of a young child inspiring adults by individually tossing beach swept starfish back into the sea. The child corrects their elders about making a difference. In this post (https://cce.sonoma.edu/sites/cce/files/keith_morton_starfish_story_deconstruction.pdf) Morton (n.d.) implores us to avoid using this story or, at the very least, contextualize it by acknowledging how it reinforces stereotypes and avoids the complexity that student activists grapple with daily.

References

Alonso, J. (2024, June 18). Are students who protested losing out on job opportunities? *Inside Higher Education.* www.insidehighered.com/news/students/careers/2024/06/18/student-protesters-face-scrutiny-job-search

American Association of Colleges & Universities (AAC&U). (n.d.). Civic engagement VALUE rubric. www.aacu.org/initiatives/value-initiative/value-rubrics/value-rubrics-civic-engagement

American Psychological Association (APA). (2024). Civic engagement. www.apa.org/education-career/undergrad/civic-engagement

Baxter Magolda, M. B., & King, P. M. (2012). Special issue: Assessing meaning making and self-authorship: Theory, research, and application. *ASHE Higher Education Report*, *38*(3), 1–138. https://doi.org/10.1002/aehe.20003

Biddix, J. P. (2014). Development through dissent: Campus activism as civic learning. *New Directions in Higher Education*, *167*, 73–85. https://doi.org/10.1002/he.20106

Cann, C., & DeMeulenaere, E. (2020). *The activist academic: Engaged scholarship for resistance, hope and social change*. Myers Education Press.

Chittum, J. R., Enke, K. A. E., & Finley, A. P. (2022). *The effects of community-based and civic engagement in higher education*. American Association of Colleges & Universities (AAC&U). https://dgmg81phhvh63.cloudfront.net/content/user-photos/Research/PDFs/Effects-of-Community-based-and-Civic-Engagement.pdf

Conner, J. (2023). "We are missing our lessons to teach you one:" Youth activists on the frontlines of climate justice. In P. C. Rosier (Ed.), *Environmental justice in North America* (pp. 355–384). Routledge. https://doi.org/10.4324/9781003214380-15

Dickey, C. (2024, June 5). The specter of "indoctrination." *The Chronicle of Higher Education*. www.chronicle.com/article/the-specter-of-indoctrination?utm_source=Iterable&utm_medium=email&utm_campaign=campaign_10168016_nl_Academe-Today_date_20240617&cid=at&source=&sourceid=

Farago, F., Swadener, B. B., Richter, J., Eversman, K. A., & Roca-Servat, D. (2018). Local to global justice: Roles of student activism in higher education, leadership development, and community engagement. *Alberta Journal of Educational Research*, *64*(2), 154–172. https://doi.org/10.55016/ojs/ajer.v64i2.56382

Finley, A. (2023). *The career-ready graduate: What employers say about the difference college makes*. American Association of College & Universities (AAC&U). https://dgmg81phhvh63.cloudfront.net/content/user-photos/Research/PDFs/AACU-2023-Employer-Report.pdf

Flett, G. L. (2022). An introduction, review, and conceptual analysis of mattering as an essential construct and an essential way of life. *Journal of Psychoeducational Assessment*, *40*(1), 3–36. https://doi.org/10.1177/07342829211057640

Freire, P. (1970/1986). *Pedagogy of the oppressed* (M. B. Ramos, Trans.). Continuum.

Gervais, M. (2023). *The first rule of mastery: Stop worrying about what people think of you*. Harvard Business Review Press.

Haidar, E. H., & Kettles, C. E. (2024, May 24). Outrage at decision to deny diplomas to 13 pro-Palestine students overshadows Harvard commencement. *The Harvard Crimson.* www.thecrimson.com/article/2024/5/24/commencement-overshadowed-proPalestine-outrage/

Harrison, L. M., & Mather, P. C. (2017). Making meaning of student activism: Student activist and administrator perspectives. *Mid-Western Educational Researcher*, *29*(2), 117–135. https://scholarworks.bgsu.edu/mwer/vol29/iss2/3

Hemer, K. M., & Reason, R. D. (2021). Civic learning for dissent: Developing students' activist orientation. *Journal of College Student Development*, *62*(1), 37–54. https://doi.org/10.1353/csd.2021.0003

Hoffman, G. D., & Mitchell, T. D. (2016). Making diversity "everyone's business": A discourse analysis of institutional responses to student activism for equity and inclusion. *Journal of Diversity in Higher Education*, *9*(3), 277–289. https://doi.org/10.1037/dhe0000037

Iowa and Minnesota Campus Compact (IMCC). (n.d.). Social change wheel 2.0 toolkit. https://seed-coalition.org/wp-content/uploads/2024/06/Social-Change-Wheel-2.0-Toolkit-05.08.2021.pdf

Jacoby, B. (2017). The new student activism: Supporting students as agents of social change. *Journal of College and Character*, *18*(1), 1–8. https://doi.org/10.1080/2194587X.2016.1260479

Jay, M. (2024). *The twentysomething treatment*. Simon & Schuster.

Keeling, R. P., & Associates. (2004). *Learning reconsidered: A campus-wide focus on the student experience*. The National Association of Student Personnel Administrators (NASPA) and College Student Educators International (ACPA). www.naspa.org/images/uploads/main/Learning_Reconsidered_Report.pdf

Kezar, A., Acuña Avilez, A., Drivalas, Y., & Wheaton, M. M. (2017). Building social change oriented leadership capacity among student organizations: Developing students and campuses simultaneously. *New Directions in Student Leadership*, *155*, 45–57. https://doi.org/10.1002/yd.20249

Kornbluh, M., Davis, A. L., Hoyt, L. T., Simpson, S. B., Cohen, A. K., & Ballard, P. J. (2022). Exploring civic behaviors amongst college students in a year of national unrest. *Journal of Community Psychology*, *50*(7), 2950–2972. https://doi.org/10.1002/jcop.22808

Kuh, G. D. (2008). *High-impact educational practices: What they are, who has access to them, and why they matter*. Association of American Colleges & Universities (AAC&U). www.aacu.org/publication/high-impact-educational-practices-what-they-are-who-has-access-to-them-and-why-they-matter.

Linder, C. (2019). Strategies for supporting student activists as leaders. *New Directions for Student Leadership*, *2019*(161), 89–96. https://doi.org/10.1002/yd.20323

Linder, C., Myers, J. S., Riggle, C., & Lacy, M. (2016). From margins to mainstream: Social media as a tool for campus sexual violence activism.

Journal of Diversity in Higher Education, *9*(3), 231–244. https://doi.org/10.1037/dhe0000038

Linder, C., Quaye, S. J., Lange, A. C., Evans, M. E., & Stewart, T. J. (2020). *Identity-based student activism: Power and oppression on college campuses*. Routledge.

Linder, C., Quaye, S. J., Stewart, T. J., Okello, W. K., & Roberts, R. E. (2019). "The whole weight of the world on my shoulders:" Power, identity, and student activism. *Journal of College Student Development 60*(5), 527–542. https://doi.org/10.1353/csd.2019.0048

Martin, G. L., Williams, B. M., Green, B., & Smith, M. J. (2019). Reframing activism as leadership. *New Directions in Student Leadership*, 161, 9–24. https://doi.org/10.1002/yd.20317

McCarron, G. P., Chen, C. W., April, J., & LaMagdeleine, I. (2024). An exploratory study of the relationship between college student activists' labor and their subjective well-being: Perspectives from a U.S. Institution. *Journal of American College Health*, 1–10. Online First. https://doi.org/10.1080/07448481.2024.2338409

McCarron, G. P., Chen, C. W., Blanton, S., Guerrieri, G., Lucioni, R. G., Gurung, E., Sreevals, A., & Enciu, J. (2023). College student activists' perceptions of mattering to campus educators. *Journal of Student Affairs Research and Practice*, *61*(3), 1–17. https://doi.org/10.1080/19496591.2023.2201195

Morgan, D. L., Zilvinskis, J., & Dugan, B. (2021). Opening the activism and postsecondary education black box: Relating high-impact practices and student identity with activist behaviors. *Journal of Political Science Education*, *17*(1), 55–78. https://doi.org/10.1080/15512169.2019.1612248

Morton, K. (n.d.). Starfish hurling and community service. https://cce.sonoma.edu/sites/cce/files/keith_morton_starfish_story_deconstruction.pdf

Nicolazzo, Z. (2016). "Just go in looking good:" The resilience, resistance, and kinship-building of Trans college students. *Journal of College Student Development*, *57*(5), 538–556. https://doi.org/10.1353/csd.2016.0057

Owen, J. E. (2016). Fostering critical reflection: Moving from a service to a social justice paradigm. *New Directions for Student Leadership*, *150*, 37–48. https://doi.org/10.1002/yd.20169

Owen, J. E., McCarron, G. P., & Chen, C. W. (2022). "Never 'because of', always 'in spite of':" Implications of the culturally relevant leadership learning model for student social justice activists. *Journal of Leadership Studies*, *16*(3), 45–50. https://doi.org/10.1002/jls.21820

Pierce, J. E. (2021). *Belonging through dissent: A national study of student activist sense of belonging and institutional integration* (Publication No. 28411444) [Doctoral dissertation, University of Georgia].

Schwartz, S. E. O., Benoit, L., Clayton, S., Parnes, M. F., Swenson, L., & Lowe, S. R. (2023). Climate change anxiety and mental health: Environmental activism as buffer. *Current Psychology*, *42*(20), 16708–16721. https://doi.org/10.1007/s12144-022-02735-6

Shenberger, M. A. (2022). *Undergraduate student activism and engagement in the leadership process* (Publication No. 2740276154) [Doctoral dissertation, Florida State University].

Steinberg, K. S., Hatcher, J. A., & Bringle, R. G. (2011) Civic-minded graduate: A north star. *Michigan Journal of Community Service Learning*, *18*(1), 19–33. https://hdl.handle.net/1805/4592

Stewart, T. J., Linder, C., Evans, M. E., Quaye, S. J., & Lange, A. C. (2020). "You hired me to do this:" Power, identity, and student activist support. *Journal of Student Affairs Research & Practice*, *59*(1), 44–58. https://doi.org/10.1080/19496591.2020.1778486

Warnock, D. M., & Hurst, A. L. (2016). "The poor kids' table:" Organizing around an invisible and stigmatized identity in flux. *Journal of Diversity in Higher Education*, *9*(3), 261–276. https://10.1037/dhe0000029

Welch, M., & Saltmarsh, J. (2016). *Engaging higher education: Purpose, platforms, and programs for community engagement*. Routledge.

3 Who I Am Is What I Do

College Student Activists' Identities and Activism

I feel like all of my work ... at the end of the day comes down to collective liberation of all marginalized people ... . It comes down a lot to the experiences that I had and understanding the systems of oppression that have held down LGBTQ+ people ... . It's about systems that are reliant on gender norms that are telling men, women, non-binary folks, people who fall in this vast, vast array of identities. It's about systems that don't acknowledge your existence or support your existence. They don't give you equal access to health care, to housing, and to protections in the job place. When I started to realize that at young age—pretty much like eighth, ninth grade—that's when I start to get more interested in advocacy work.

I remember when I first came out, I felt comfortable holding hands with my boyfriend at the time. We were walking in downtown. I lived in a city, very diverse. I was walking downtown. I remember three cars circling us, throwing [stuff] at us, and yelling out ... . Saying all these awful things in those moments, it was hurtful, and it was scary. I didn't know if I was going to make it out alive, but in those instances and moving forward, I started to realize the deeper issues at hand. We have a system that supports these types of actions, support this type of thoughts because our public school system doesn't teach about queer history. It doesn't teach about the humaneness behind queer identity. There's systems that perpetuate that. Like I said, literally 100 times already, whether it be healthcare, housing, jobs, things like that. I think a lot of my experience comes down to those hard situations that I've gone through.

I wouldn't change it at the end of the day. My biggest thing about the way I organize is that I would much rather that I experienced this so that I know how it impacts people ... . I don't know how it impacts everyone if it were also different, but I'd rather have this happened to

DOI: 10.4324/9781003481010-3

> *me because I know the reality of it. That means I can advocate hard like hell for this to end on both within systems and within society. That's a little bit about the work that I do and the background on how we got involved in advocacy work. A lot of it comes from that life experience.*—Masvusi

Masvusi, the student activist who shared the narrative above, was a 19-year-old college sophomore at the time of our interview and identified as a gay, White man from a low-income, food-insecure home. His story highlights the role of identity as the primary motivation for engaging in activism and underscores the personal dynamics that drive student engagement in societal change.

Introduction

The purpose of this chapter is to explore how college student activists perceive the relationship between their identity and organizational and social change-making. Linder and colleagues (2020) articulated that college students engaging in identity-based activism named student identity (i.e., who they were) as a driver. Thus, with this framing in mind, as a collective of students, educators, administrators, and allies, we hope to make meaning of how the college student activists who participated in our study perceived the connection between their identity and their activism. We do this with the essential aim of sharing and re-imagining pathways for supporting college student activist well-being. First, this chapter explores the meaning of identity and the more complex nature of intersectionality in student activist work. Next, literature examining factors that contribute to youth and young adults' sociopolitical development will be considered. The literature review closes with a journey into the relationship between specific identities (e.g., race, sexual orientation) and activism. Findings from the study described in Chapter One of this volume will be shared, which will center if and how participants' identity and intersections of identity were connected to their motivations to serve as change agents. This chapter closes with a discussion of the implications for research and practice relevant to student activist well-being and key recommendations via the "Scholarship in Action" section.

Literature Review

Identity and Intersectionality

Fundamentally, the American Psychological Association (APA, n.d.) notes that identity is "an individual's sense of self defined by (a) a set of physical, psychological, and interpersonal characteristics that is not wholly shared with any other person and (b) a range of affiliations (e.g., ethnicity) and social roles" (para. 1). Yet, beyond this definition, the notion of "identity" is much broader and more complex given scholarly and practical contexts. Relevant to the work of this chapter and volume, college student development literature has evolved to underscore that individuals hold multiple identities (e.g., race, ethnicity, immigration status, sexual orientation, gender, ability, age) that—depending on a range of variable micro-contexts as well as ever-present macro structures of power and historically dominant ideologies—can be oppressed or privileged (Abes et al., 2007; Duran et al., 2024; Jones & Abes, 2013). Thus, identities are not experienced in a vacuum and are subject to a host of social constructs and systems that impact both how an individual sees themselves and *is seen* and valued in the larger community (Abes et al., 2007; Jones & McEwen, 2000). To this point, Amiot and colleagues (2007, 2018) noted that the experience of identity can be configured differently depending on an individual's cognitive processes: Individuals can categorize, compartmentalize, or integrate their multiple identities. Categorization speaks to an individual seeing one identity as salient while excluding others, compartmentalization enables an individual to value multiple identities that are kept separate and activated based on social contexts, while integration allows for a supra-identity via which multiple identities are equally important (Amiot et al., 2007, 2018). Of special note here is that this relationship between identity, nexus of identities, identity configurations, perception, social construction, and systemic influences is folded into intersectionality.

Intersectionality, originally inspired by Black feminist leaders and activists such as Anna Julia Cooper (1892), was conceptualized formally by Crenshaw (1989) as a legal framework to call out the explicit marginalization experienced by Black women at the juncture of systemic sexist and racist oppression. Applied in broader work, intersectionality emphasizes the matrices of domination (Collins, 2000, 2009; Collins & Bilge, 2020) by acknowledging the "overlapping and conflicting dynamics of race, gender, class, sexuality, nation, and other inequalities" (Cho et al., 2013, p. 788). Given the influence of intersectionality on students' overall identity development (Duran & Jones, 2019) and that this chapter specifically speaks to the role of college student activists' identities and threats to those identities as motivation for action, we cannot consider identity and activism without also considering the connection between intersectionality and social change. In the following section, we will briefly discuss the body of literature centering identity and activism, paying special attention to elements of intersectionality in that literature.

Identity and Activism

In their separate studies on social justice youth development (SJYD), Ginwright and Cammarota (2002) and Watts and colleagues (2003) offered ecological explorations of youth development in an effort to explain what drove youth and young adults to social action. Though varied in their ecological approaches, both models spoke to how youth enact change in response to the realization of privilege and oppressive systems. Thus, these scholars made the case that identity and recognition of inequity spark a "critical consciousness" (Freire, 1973)—an awareness of systemic forces' roles in promoting and limiting opportunities based on identity. In short, emerging adults' unique positioning within systems of privilege and oppression—and their awareness of such systems—play a role in shaping how they engage in social action and sociopolitical development. Ginwright and Cammarota as well as Watts and colleagues' work was echoed by Guerrero and colleagues (2021) who examined emerging adults' perceived motivations and barriers to social justice engagement as well as the role of identity. Via analysis of the lived experiences of 30 participants, the team found that factors such as proximity to the social issue shaped engagement: Identity *and* reflection on identity catalyzed involvement and engagement in social action. Similarly, in a national study of nearly 900 individuals, Hope and colleagues (2019) explored how experiences of institutional and cultural racial discrimination linked to Black adolescents and emerging adults' orientations toward activism in the Black community. The researchers found that Black adolescents and emerging adults' experiences of institutional racism and perceptions of others viewing Black people negatively connected to a greater high-risk activism orientation. In other words, perceptions of individual *and* systemic marginalization served as catalysts for centering social change. This finding underscores Linder et al.'s (2020) observation that the student activist narrative is often one of marginalized communities doing the work of activism as a liberatory act of resistance while *simultaneously* struggling through the muck of power dynamics and oppressive structures within social systems. To this point, Bjornsen-Ramig and Kissinger (2018) emphasized the risks to well-being for student activists who engaged in activism that was personal and proximal to their struggle.

The story of resistance and struggle with respect to college student identity and activism was reflected in Asakura's (2017) work, which explored identity in the context of high school and college youth who identified as lesbian, gay, bisexual, trans, and queer. Asakura found that activism was catalyzed by the pain of social marginalization *and* that participants spoke to the power of asserting personal agency as a vehicle for un-silencing their marginalized identities. Supporting Asakura's discovery, in their work examining National Survey of Student Engagement (NSSE) data focused on the responses of over 3000 post-secondary students' sentiments on activist behavior, Morgan and colleagues (2021) noted that students who identified as Black or queer were significantly more likely to participate in activism compared with other students in the NSSE sample. While the data did not explicitly ask "why" these students were more active, the findings do suggest that those with minoritized or marginalized identities were more so moved to action. Aligned with this point and broadened to engage elements of intersectionality, Manzano and colleagues (2017) explored two students'—Alyssa and Khoa—intersectional Asian American identity consciousness and spoke to how racialized experiences served as critical incidents that informed activism and leadership. With deeper insight into intersectionality and activism work, Leigh and colleagues (2021) troubled existing research noting that it failed to speak to leadership and activism roles for Asian American women who carried other social identities. In their work, they confirmed the salience of racialized and gendered processes shaping participants' engagement and their interpretations of engagement (Leigh et al., 2021).

This brief literature review of work focused on identity and youth/student activism underscores the unquestionable link between identity and motivations for activism and social change movements. Our aim with this chapter is to expand on the work above and offer a glimpse into the lived experiences of college student activists through their own words. At the onset of this chapter, we connected to Masvusi's voice as he offered that: "I think a lot of my experience comes down to those hard situations that I've gone through." Yes, we embrace him and the many dozens of other college student activists who spoke to how identities (and threat to those identities) shaped their passion for advocacy, activism, and organizing. In the following section we hear from these activists and make meaning in the context of our hope to understand how these college student activists perceived the connection between identity and activism.

Findings

For many of the college student activists who participated in our study, identity and intersections of multiple identities were deeply connected to their motivations to serve as change agents. A subset of these students for whom activism was born from experiences of marginalized identities, remarkably also leveraged their dominant identities to serve as advocates for those who felt silenced (e.g., a White, gay man advocating for Black transgender individuals). Below, we elaborate on identity as motivation and the role of dominant identities in activism.

College Student Activists' Identities and Motivation for Activism

Across the unique stories shared by the 119 college student activists who participated in the work scaffolding this volume, the connection between identity as motivation for activism was a constant thread. Clara C., a Latina woman who was completing her graduate studies at the time she spoke with us, reflected deeply on this connection with respect to her work in immigration rights spaces and her own identity as an immigrant. Clara shared the following:

> Immigration … is the issue that is most dear to me. And, of course, being a first-gen immigrant and going through the process and being an outcome of a system that has been broken and designed to oppress and marginalize people that carry my skin tone here … I have found myself … diving deeper into what advocacy means, but also understanding … my sense of belonging … in the movement.

Aligned with Clara's thoughts on personal identity and race, Sherry, a Black woman completing her junior year at the time of her interview, made similar connections between identity and her activism. Sherry offered that:

> it took just talking with family because obviously my family is Black. They understand what the Black community goes through. It's just like talking to them about how I felt. … Just knowing that there were people before me who fought for my rights and fought for the generations after them just made me … . I just thought I would do the same thing, fight for the generations after me. That's why I'm in.

For participant Lucy, "getting in" the fight was also incredibly personal. Lucy, who identified as a White woman and a member of the LGBTQ+ community, struggled relentlessly at her highly conservative Catholic university to create a safe space and catalyze institutional respect for fellow students identifying as LGBTQ+. In her interview, Lucy shared that her aim was to support a "group of people who were like me and who were in the same boat." A similar aim held true for participant Benjamin. Benjamin identified as a White, non-binary, gay man—and like Lucy—they pulled from their own identity to support those in the LGBTQ+ community. Benjamin described their identity development and journey to activism as follows:

> So, I started very young. I went to an activist camp … which is a local LGBT organization for LGBT youth. And we had this like lesson on inequality under capitalism, and that shook me and helped me to start understanding the world outside of myself.

The notion of finding strength to fight because of experiences of identity was also part of Dana's narrative as she relayed the stories of how her salient identities formed. Dana identified as an adult learner, White woman, immigrant, and refugee. Her experiences as a young girl whose childhood was cut short in a war-torn Eastern European country came together to create a blend of immigrant and refugee identity that motivated her desire to advocate for children's rights and the rights of military members in need. In reflecting on the connections between her past, her identities, and her activism, Dana offered the following:

> That [witnessing of war and bloodshed] stunted my growth and reshaped it into … I don't know how to say it. Reshaped it to be more open, to care for others. I don't know. Maybe empathy that overly shaped … . Growing up with that added more heart to me.

Dana, Lucy, Benjamin, Sherry, and Clara described authentically the bridge between their own identities and their activism work. While, undoubtedly, elements of intersectionality were part of their stories, following, we explore the voices of several college student activist participants who made explicit reference to intersectionality, systems, and their activism.

Intersectionality

As noted in the introduction of this chapter, intersectionality lays bare issues of systemic marginalization and oppression by highlighting the "overlapping and conflicting dynamics of race, gender, class, sexuality, nation, and other inequalities" (Cho et al., 2013, p. 788). For many of the college student activists in our study, intersectionality was a well-understood phenomenon, which they related to their own identities and motivations for activism. For example, Penny, a Latina woman who had felt marginalized due to the intersections of multiple minoritized identities, shared that "[getting involved] was inevitable" after having experienced an entanglement of racism, sexism, and classism in a flawed and systemically compromised society.

Akin to Penny's story, Shay's narrative was one of feeling the systemic oppressions that came from holding multiple marginalized identities as a woman, person of color, and member of the LGBTQ+ community. In her interview, Shay offered the following when commenting on why she was involved in her current activism work:

> I feel like it's probably a byproduct just because my intersections of my identity with like, definitely like racial issues and racial justice, talking about sexism and advocating for women and like the LGBTQ+ community, cuz those are all things that directly affect me, impact me.

Echoing Shay, college student activist Phil, who identified as a Latino man and was completing doctoral studies, spoke to the links between identity and activism, as well as intersectionality, but he took the conversation one step further, highlighting systems as follows:

> I think the issues that I focus more intently on are the ones that are in relation to the identities I hold or in relation to an experience that is impacting to a friend or loved one. So, what I mean by that is when it comes to my identities, I'm a person of color, I'm first generation, a member of the LGBTQ+ community. I'm a doctoral student. And so, a lot of the systematic challenges that I tried to address are usually directed to the identities.

Phil, Shay, and Penny offered a glimpse of their activism work at the intersections of their identities in the context of larger, systemic marginalization. Via their stories, we can tease apart how these activists perceived the relationship between who they are and their activism.

College Student Activists' Leveraging of Dominant Identities in Activism

In discussing identity's connection to activism, several study participants expanded their stories to share that, though they carried minoritized identities that catalyzed action, they also claimed privileged identities that granted them capacity to make change in service to those more silenced. For example, Thomas, a college senior who identified as a White, gay man, also used his privileged identities to catalyze change and to speak for those Black transgender individuals in the LGBTQ+ community who felt erased. Thomas shared the following:

> Specifically, I like to focus on areas within the LGBTQ community. I'm a gay man myself so it … hits home a little bit more for me. Specifically, Black trans lives has been a very big one recently that I feel even in the current climate aren't being heard the right way that they should be and as a White man I have a little bit easier of a voice, and a little bit better of a platform …
>
> Being a gay man, I came out with family … I kind of started to recognize that people around me didn't have the same ability to come out to the people that they loved. And that kind of just got the ball rolling. To start recognizing that there are people in situations, similar to mine, that have a much different outcome.

Like Thomas, Karen—a biracial (Mexican and White) woman—not only spoke about the centrality of her identity as a person of color in wanting to make change for folks of color, but she also named her privileged economic context as a member of the upper middle class as an avenue for change. Note how she intentionally leverages the privileged aspects of her identity to benefit her community. Karen went on to share the following:

> Also just being a woman of color in a predominantly White area, just having that experience and living through that. Also, seeing how much privilege I have in comparison to other people who share similar identities to me has made me … [I] realize that I have to use my position of privilege to help those communities.
>
> We have so much access in the world to information and the more I learn the more I just felt that I couldn't just sit back with all of this privilege and let it go to waste living for myself … . I've always known this is going to be my life's work. I've always known that it was going to be difficult. I've just always come from such a place of privilege that I've never had to directly interact with it.

Echoing some of Karen's sentiments, Phil—a Latino man—underscored the systemic challenges with respect to his intersecting identities but also the spaces in which he recognized his own privileges as avenues for making change supporting others who suffered even more marginalization. Phil articulated the following thoughts:

> … a lot of the systematic or challenges that I tried to address are usually directed to the identities I have, right? But when looking at the issues that may not directly impact my identity, or that I may have privileges and I look at my colleagues and or my peers, or my friends and family, who are now getting different systems, where I want to support them in. So, healthcare, for example, I have good health right now. However, my grandfather the diabetic, and so I know when it comes to insulin and how expensive that is, and so, there are topics that in terms of activism and advocacy that directly impact my identities, which I think I have more involvement in. And for those that don't impact my identities but impact the identities of my friends and colleagues, I also tried to have some form and engaging with that, to support them.

Phil, Karen, and Thomas shared a meaningful perspective on the "both/and" of identity and activism with respect to marginalized and privileged identities that can exist and be motivations simultaneously. This observation expands the discourse of identity and activism from a monolithic one focusing on pain and purpose, and grows the conversation to one of community and collective care. While the idea of community will be engaged more deeply in Chapter Five of this volume, below, we discuss the findings above and connect to implications for practice and future research.

Discussion and Implications: College Student Activists' Well-Being

Discussion

Our findings underscored that identities and intersections of identities were deeply connected to college student activists' motivations to serve as organization, community, and global changemakers in spaces proximal to their struggles. These findings converge with Manzano and colleagues' (2017) discoveries, which noted that not only did identity inform participants' activism regarding racial and ethnic concerns, but it also motivated solidarity with larger communities. This notion of building broader personal and community agency in response to identity-based motivation is also consistent with Asakura's (2017) observations. Remarkably, beyond discussions of singular identity motivations, participants in the study also commented on how they perceived their activism and themselves in the context of intersectionality and the systemic oppressions they experienced. Phil, Shay, and Penny all spoke to the mosaic of their identities subject to structural marginalization and the direct linkage to social action. They—directly or indirectly—articulated that their identities did not express themselves in silos but were best understood with attention to social constructs. Via their narratives, Phil, Shay, and Penny gave voice to the work of Abes and colleagues (2007), Cho and collaborators (2013), and Jones and McEwen (2000). Elaborating on the intersectionality discussion, some of the college student activists represented in this chapter not only honed their activism *because* of experiences of marginalized identity, but they also *leveraged their dominant identities* to serve as advocates for those whose voices could not be amplified. This finding recalls observations offered by

Duran and colleagues (2024) and Jones and Abes (2013) who shared that individuals' multiple identities could be oppressed or privileged depending on context.

Interestingly, as we reflect on the themes and findings discussed above, we begin to notice a pattern emerge in the context of participants' perceptions of the relationship between identity and their activism, which emphasizes linkages to student activist well-being. If we return to the conceptual framework for this volume outlined in Chapter One and in McCarron and colleagues (2024), we recall that, in their conceptualization of subjective well-being (SWB), Diener and collaborators (2009) noted that SWB "reflects a general evaluation of a person's life" (p. 71) and is comprised of four somewhat correlated components that can nurture SWB: Pleasant emotions, unpleasant emotions, global life judgments, and domain satisfaction. As noted in Table 3.1, several sub-components comprise each of these four SWB facets. In our work, participants often associated marginalization of their identities with unpleasant emotions (e.g., Clara's sadness about the journey of the immigrant community for which she advocated) that seemed to catalyze the resulting positive life judgments oriented around action-taking and change-making (e.g., Clara's feeling of belonging and sense of purpose).

Of note, is that this same pattern held for most students' stories shared in this chapter—pleasant emotions or positive life judgments started with sadness, anger, or worry (e.g., unpleasant emotions) that related to feeling minoritized and/or seeing others being silenced. This observation finds commonality with the youth development work of Ginwright and Cammarota (2002) and Watts and colleagues (2003), who described youth participants enacting change in response to the recognition of privilege and oppressive systems. In a sense, negative

Table 3.1 Subjective Well-Being Components and Sample Sub-Components

Pleasant Emotions	*Unpleasant Emotions*	*Life Judgments*	*Domain Satisfaction*
Joy	Sadness	Life satisfaction	Marriage
Contentment	Anger	Fulfillment	Work
Happiness	Worry	Meaning	Health
Love	Stress	Success	Leisure

Note: Adapted from Diener and colleagues (2009).

SWB "indicators" informed or primed positive indicators as part of the motivation process. Yet, we offer this bit of analysis with extreme caution given that, for college student activists writ large, there may be no positive or happy ending to the social movement work. Here we highlight the voices of participants who, because of their marginalized identities, carried disproportionate burdens as activists. Linder and colleagues (2020) made clear the weariness associated with identity-driven activism and the associated detriment to well-being—a reflection supported by Bjornsen-Ramig and Kissinger (2018) and Hope and colleagues (2019). Thus, as we unpack college student activists' perceptions of the relationship between their identities and their activism, we have a duty to keep this nuance at the forefront of discussion.

Implications for Practice and Future Research

For many institutions of higher education, the notion of "supporting college student activists" may be fraught given that student activists often focus on university policies and practices as spaces for change and, as such, may perceive favor or disfavor based on whether they advocate for external issues or campus-based concerns (Linder, 2019; McCarron et al., 2023). Yet, the "student" part of "college student activist" falls squarely under the purview of colleges and universities charged with teaching and learning. This chapter is not a rallying cry demanding that institutions support students' activism agendas. We are simply reminding ourselves and our larger community of the necessity for institutions of higher education to care about the well-being of college student activists as individuals—*as students*—on a development journey (McCarron et al., 2023, 2024). As we consider student activists' identities and activism, we call on colleagues to hold dear an understanding of the salience of identity, the complexities of intersectionality, the many vectors of oppression, and place of power (Collins, 2000). This understanding is certainly critical for engaging student activists but is also critical for the holistic development and purposeful orientation of all students.

Going forward, we ask colleagues to help students build bridges between their sense of self and their place in the world, and to offer scaffolding toward students' deeper understanding of purpose. The participants in this study were clear—Who I Am Is What I Do—and, as such, at institutions of higher learning, we must support students in discovering who they are without the trappings of our own assumptions. Thus, we encourage colleagues to engage in formal and informal reflexive practice aimed at auditing implicit and explicit biases around care for college *student* activists given students' identities and their own. We encourage considering the following reflection questions: How are we working to help students make meaning of their identities and their pasts in service to the future? How are we partnering with students to strengthen their agency for long-term change-making? Do these partnership efforts differ depending on students' identities? Are we creating spaces for students to engage meaningfully with peers and mentors around identity to support community-building? Are we encouraging the development of critical consciousness as students shift from self-awareness to social action? How do we understand intersectionality and the context for students' pressures, purpose, and obligations? Are we creating spaces for interrogation of privileged and oppressed identities in context as well as more deeply engaging the role of allies?

For faculty, staff, and administrators, the goal of asking questions like those above is to hold space for students as whole people first—people with multiple and intersecting identities, which may cause pain, endanger well-being, inspire action, and bring purpose. As educators, we must take in the full arc of well-being and journey with student activists as they visit, revise, reject, and return to the many facets of well-being—those offered by Diener and colleagues (2009) and beyond. The "beyond," especially, offers a robust opening for future research exploring the linkages between college student activists' identities and activism.

As we look to additional spaces of inquiry, we wonder about broadening our understanding of identity, activism, and well-being by leveraging student development theory to map how students' affective and cognitive complexity might shift the types of well-being approaches required. For example, how might students who are further along in their epistemological and intellectual development describe the intersections of identity and activism work and the supports needed to thrive? Additionally, future research might take a longitudinal approach to exploring the nexus of college student activists' identities and connections to activism as a way to understand changes in students' purpose and to identify spaces for meaningful conversations with educators about fulfillment, meaning, and other life judgments. Regardless of the nature of scholarly work, the aim should be consistent: Fostering knowledge that helps college *student* activists fortify the bridge between who they are and what they do.

Conclusion

The purpose of this chapter was to understand how college student activists perceived the relationship between their identities and their activism. We briefly discussed relevant literature pertaining to how we understand identity and intersectionality in student activist work. We also considered scholarship exploring the relationship between specific identities (e.g., race, sexual orientation) and activism. This chapter's findings pointed to two major themes: Identity and intersections of multiple identities were deeply connected to college student activists' motivations to serve as change agents in spaces proximal to their own struggles; and though their activism was born from experiences of marginalized identities, many of these same students leveraged their dominant identities to serve as advocates for those who felt silenced. In the context of college student activism and SWB, these findings speak to the unpleasant emotions (e.g., anger, sadness) associated with minoritized experiences at the individual and systemic levels that often propelled students into positive life judgments such as finding purpose and meaning in activism work. Understanding the nuances of identity, activism, and well-being is essential to engendering constructive dialogues and reflexive practice across institutions of higher education that center the "student" in college student activism and aim to engage students in the learning journey toward purpose and meaningful aims. The participants in this chapter essentially articulated that Who They Are Is What They Do; as such, we call on colleges, universities, and educator allies to mimic this mantra: If an institution identifies as a center of learning and holistic student development, then the "doing" of such must follow.

Scholarship in Action
Identity, Activism, and College Student Activist Well-Being

Thought Questions:

For students: How do you think about your multiple and intersecting identities in the context of your activism? What are some additional ways you might explore this linkage in an effort to evolve your personal development and your practice as an activist? What is your purpose?

For staff/practitioners: How are you helping students make meaning of their identities and their pasts in service to the future? In what ways are you creating spaces for students to engage meaningfully with peers and mentors around identity? How are you encouraging the development of critical consciousness as students shift from self-awareness to social action?

For faculty: In what ways are you partnering with college student activists to strengthen their agency for long-term change-making? In what ways are you engaging with students around self-understanding and motivation/purpose for change? If you are not, what is holding you back from taking this step with students? How might you seek out partnerships or support to help understand and overcome potential resistance or concerns?

For community partners: As you engage with college student activists in your teams and organizations, how might you take steps to understand the role of students' identities in their activism work as an avenue toward helping to strengthen their sense of agency and purpose?

For researchers: Are there ways in which you can deepen your own understanding of how your multiple and intersecting identities show up in the way you think and write about college student change-making and agency? In what ways might assumptions and biases in how you consider college student activists and activism shape your research questions and approach?

Resources for Additional Learning:

Websites:

The CLDE Framework for College Civic Learning and Democracy Engagement serves as a useful model in helping students and educators understand what students should

gain from civic and democracy engagement. The framework encourages students' reflection on their civic identities, experiences, and responsibilities.
www.collegeciviclearning.org/learning-framework

Podcasts:

Identity-Based Activism (2022, September 7): Student Affairs Now
https://studentaffairsnow.com/identity-based-activism/

Conferences:

NASPA – Student Affairs Administration in Higher Education Well-Being in Higher Education
www.naspa.org/events/well-beinginhighered

Books:

Dabbs, K. (2024). *You belong here: The power of being seen, heard, and valued on your own terms*. Berrett-Koehler Publishers.

Everyone feels like an outsider at some point in their life. This book suggests that, instead of feeling excluded, many hide their authentic selves and let others define their identities. This volume explores four aspects of identity that lead us closer to authenticity: A lived identity, a learned identity, a lingering identity, and a loved identity.

Linder, C., Quaye, S., Lange, A., Evans, M. E., & Stewart, T. J. (2020). *Identity-based student activism: Power and oppression on college campuses*. Routledge.

This book explores the experiences of students engaged in identity-based activism as it relates to racism, sexism, homophobia, transphobia, ableism, and other forms of oppression. Grounded by a national study on student activism and the authors' combined 40 years of experience working in higher education, this volume uses a critical, power-conscious lens to unpack the history of identity-based activism, relationships between activists and administrators, and student activism as labor.

Muñoz, S. M. (2015). *Identity, social activism, and the pursuit of higher education: The journey stories of undocumented and unafraid community activists*. Peter Lang.

As the topic of immigration has become increasingly volatile in the United States, undocumented college students may play a central role in mobilizing a pro-immigration agenda. This volume includes "journey stories" of community activists who are undocumented and shares narratives related to advocating for the Development, Relief, and Education for Alien Minors (DREAM) Act.

Articles:

Linder, C. (2019). Power-conscious and intersectional approaches to supporting student activists: Considerations for learning and development. *Journal of Diversity in Higher Education, 12*(1), 17–26. https://doi.org/10.1037/dhe0000082

Taylor, R. M., Burr, K. H., Stroup, N. R., & McCloud, L. I. (2023). "Speaking up when I disagree:" Exploring college student activism and openness to diversity and challenge. *Journal of Diversity in Higher Education*. Online First. https://doi.org/10.1037/dhe0000484

Classroom Activities:

Consider engaging in a thoughtful conversation with students using the Social Identity Wheel, which encourages students to reflect on their social identities and how those identities are more or less salient depending on context and personal histories. Facilitators can also engage in a discussion about identity with respect to motivations and purpose for social change. The Wheel activity page as well as facilitation guidance can be found at https://sites.lsa.umich.edu/equitable-teaching/social-identity-wheel/

References

Abes, E. S., Jones, S. R., & McEwen, M. K. (2007). Reconceptualizing the model of multiple dimensions of identity: The role of meaning-making capacity in the construction of multiple identities. *Journal of College Student Development*, *48*(1), 1–22. https://doi.org/10.1353/csd.2007.0000

American Psychological Association (APA). (n.d.). *APA dictionary of psychology*. APA. https://dictionary.apa.org/identity

Amiot, C. E., De La Sablonnière, R., Terry, D. J., & Smith, J. (2007). Integration of social identities in the self: Toward a cognitive-developmental model. *Personality and Social Psychology Review*, *11*(4), 364–388. https://doi.org/10.1177/1088868307304091

Amiot, C. E., Doucerain, M. M., Zhou, B., & Ryder, A. (2018). Cultural identity dynamics: Capturing changes in cultural identities over time and their intraindividual organization. *European Journal of Social Psychology*, *48*, 629–644. https://doi.org/10.1002/ejsp.2355

Asakura, K. (2017). Paving pathways through the pain: A grounded theory of resilience among lesbian, gay, bisexual, trans, and queer youth. *Journal of Research on Adolescence*, *27*, 521–536. https://doi.org/10.1111/jora.12291

Bjornsen-Ramig, A., & Kissinger, D. (2018). Activism and college student mental health. In M. T. Miller & D. V. Tolliver (Eds.), *Exploring the technological, societal, and institutional dimensions of college student activism* (pp. 217–237). IGI Global. https://doi.org/10.4018/978-1-5225-7274-9.ch013

Cho, S., Crenshaw, K. W., & McCall, L. (2013). Toward a field of intersectionality studies: Theory, applications, and praxis. *Signs*, *38*(4), 785–810. https://doi.org/10.1086/669608

Collins, P. H. (2000). Gender, Black feminism, and Black political economy. *The Annals of the American Academy of Political and Social Science*, *568*, 41–53. www.jstor.org/stable/1049471

Collins, P. H. (2009). *Black feminist thought: Knowledge, consciousness and the politics of empowerment*. Routledge (Original work published 2000).

Collins, P. H., & Blige, S. (2020). *Intersectionality* (2nd Ed.). Polity Press.

Cooper, A. J. (1892). *Voice from the South: By a Black woman of the South*. The Aldine Printing House.

Crenshaw, K. (1989). Demarginalizing the intersection of race and sex: A Black feminist critique of antidiscrimination doctrine, feminist theory and antiracist politics. *University of Chicago Legal Forum*, *1*(8), 139–167. http://chicagounbound.uchicago.edu/uclf/vol1989/iss1/8

Diener, E., Scollon, C. N., & Lucas, R. E. (2009). The evolving concept of subjective well-being: The multifaceted nature of happiness. In E. Diener (Ed.), *Assessing well-being : The collected works of Ed Diener* (pp. 67–100). Springer. http://doi.org/10.1007/978-90-481-2354-4

Duran, A., Abes, E. S., Stewart, D.-L., & Jones, S. R. (2024). Looking back, moving forward, and everything in between: Revisiting student development's relevance and enduring concepts. *Journal of College Student Development*, *65*(2), 121–136. https://doi.org/10.1353/csd.2024.a923524

Duran, A., & Jones, S. R. (2019). Using intersectionality in qualitative research on college student identity development: Considerations, tensions, and possibilities. *Journal of College Student Development*, *60*(4), 455–471. https://doi.org/10.1353/csd.2019.0040

Freire, P. (1973). *Education for critical consciousness* (Vol. 1). Bloomsbury Publishing.

Ginwright, S., & Cammarota, J. (2002). New terrain in youth development: The promise of a social justice approach. *Social Justice*, *29*(4), 82–95. www.jstor.org/stable/29768150

Guerrero, M., Anderson, A. J., Catlett, B. S., Sánchez, B., & Liao, C. L. (2021). Emerging adults' social justice engagement: Motivations, barriers, and social identity. *American Journal of Community Psychology*, *68*(1-2), 73–87. https://doi.org/10.1002/ajcp.12495

Hope, E. C., Gugwor, R., Riddick, K. N., & Pender, K. N. (2019). Engaged against the machine: Institutional and cultural racial discrimination and racial identity as predictors of activism orientation among Black youth. *American Journal of Community Psychology*, *63*, 61–72.

Jones, S. R., & Abes, E. S. (2013). *Identity development of college students: Advancing frameworks for multiple dimensions of identity*. John Wiley & Sons.

Jones, S. R., & McEwen, M. K. (2000). A conceptual model of multiple dimensions of identity. *Journal of College Student Development*, *41*(4), 405–414.

Leigh, E. W., Pak, K., & Phuong, J. (2021). Defining ourselves: Exploring our leader and activist identities as Asian American women doctoral students. *Journal of Diversity in Higher Education*, *14*(2), 174–188. https://doi.org/10.1037/dhe0000173

Linder, C. (2019). Power-conscious and intersectional approaches to supporting student activists: Considerations for learning and development. *Journal of Diversity in Higher Education*, *12*(1), 17–26. https://doi.org/10.1037/dhe0000082

Linder, C., Quaye, S., Lange, A., Evans, M. E., & Stewart, T. J. (2020). *Identity-based student activism: Power and oppression on college campuses*. Routledge.

Manzano, L. J., Poon, O. A., & Na, V. S. (2017). Asian American student engagement in student leadership and activism. *New Directions for Student Services*, *160*, 65–79. https://doi.org/10.1002/ss.20244/full

McCarron, G. P., Chen, C. W., April, J., & LaMagdeleine, I. (2024). An exploratory study of the relationship between college student activists' labor and their subjective well-being: Perspectives from a U.S. Institution. *Journal of American College Health*, 1–10. Online First. https://doi.org/10.1080/07448481.2024.2338409

McCarron, G. P., Chen, C. W., Blanton, S., Guerrieri, G., Lucioni, R. G., Gurung, E., Sreevals, A., & Enciu, J. (2023). College student activists' perceptions of mattering to campus educators. *Journal of Student Affairs Research and Practice*, *61*(3), 368–384. https://doi.org/10.1080/19496591.2023.2201195

Morgan, D. L., Zilvinskis, J., & Dugan, B. (2021). Opening the activism and postsecondary education black box: Relating high-impact practices and student identity with activist behaviors. *Journal of Political Science Education*, *17*(1), 55–78. https://doi.org/10.1080/15512169.2019.1612248

Watts, R. J., Williams, N. C., & Jagers, R. J. (2003). Sociopolitical development. *American Journal of Community Psychology*, *31*(1–2), 185–194.

4 Burnout

The Costs of Activism

> *We go to different organizations ... and give a presentation on definitions of consent ... the Title IX and OSARP process [refers to the student conduct office]. Sometimes, that can be very draining because one, it's a lot of information. Two, it's a lot of really heavy information, and we do share survivor stories. So that can be hard and very draining. And also when you can actively see that people in the audience aren't paying attention or taking in like what you're saying. Or if they're not actively engaged in the presentation [when] we do questions and scenarios and if no one's participating. It's like, why am I doing this? It doesn't matter if I'm getting anything out of this. And so with those, I can kind of feel myself getting burned out when I get to three or four [presentations] a week and I have a feeling that, only maybe five people out of the hundreds that we just talked to actually got something out of it. But the way to kind of honor that is knowing "okay, at least I reached some." Yeah, at least I got through to somebody and maybe they'll get through to somebody else.*—Abigail

Abigail, the participant who shared the narrative above, was a 21-year-old college student at the time of our interview. She identified as a White woman committed to combating sexual violence and advocating for women's rights. Her story illustrates how her activism led to burnout and stresses the various factors that contributed to it.

Introduction

The risk of burnout is a particularly pressing concern for college student activists. While stress is a common experience among college students (American College Health Association [ACHA], 2018;

DOI: 10.4324/9781003481010-4

Hartson et al., 2023), the impact on student activists can be significantly more pronounced due to their dual identities as both students and activists (Conner et al., 2023). Our 119 interviews with college student activists highlighted a prevalent experience of burnout, which took a toll on their mental and physical well-being. How these student activists responded to burnout varied considerably. This chapter explores the causes, symptoms, and coping mechanisms employed by these individuals when faced with burnout, shedding light on the multifaceted nature of burnout within the college student activist community.

Literature Review

A broader exploration of activist burnout, particularly within the realm of social justice and human rights (SJHR) activism, provides an essential context for this study. The scholarly examination of activists' lives is described by Gomes (1992), who conducted pioneering research exploring the perceived rewards and stresses among peace activists in the United States. Her study unveiled common stressors among these activists, including public apathy, slow progress, resource limitations, and strained relationships within the peace movement. Since then, a growing body of research has outlined the unique challenges faced by SJHR activists.

Burnout

The term "burnout" is often used to describe situations in which workers, volunteers, or activists experience temporary fatigue or stress. Freudenberger (1974) introduced the concept of vocational burnout, characterizing it as a more debilitating and enduring condition that extends beyond mere daily fatigue or stress (Maslach & Leiter, 2005). Pines (1994) later distilled the idea of burnout to "the end result of a process in which idealistic and highly committed individuals lose their spirit" (p. 381). In essence, burnout manifests as a state in which individuals who were once deeply committed to a cause, movement, or organization become mentally exhausted (Schaufeli & Buunk, 2002). As a consequence, they lose the sense of idealism and passion that initially propelled them to work toward social change (Pines, 1994). Over the past four decades, researchers have further developed this concept, characterizing burnout as a chronic condition

Table 4.1 Dimensions of Burnout Symptoms

Manifestation Type	*Description of Manifestation*
Affective	Involve shifts in mood, often associated with feelings of depression and anxiety.
Cognitive	Encompass deficits in attention, memory, and concentration.
Physical	Include health issues like headaches, high blood pressure, and various illnesses.
Behavioral	Comprise behavioral changes that impact productivity and health, ranging from increased procrastination to substance abuse.
Motivational	Relate to a diminishing drive, heightened feelings of alienation, and a sense of hopelessness.

(Maslach & Leiter, 2005) marked by a "state or process of mental exhaustion" (Schaufeli & Buunk, 2002, p. 383).

The symptoms of burnout are multifaceted. In their comprehensive review of 25 years of burnout research, Schaufeli and Buunk (2002) categorized burnout symptoms into five distinct dimensions (see Table 4.1).

Activist Burnout

Kovan and Dirkx (2003) highlighted that activists' lives are characterized by ongoing struggles, with burnout being a significant concern. Chen and Gorski (2015) distinguished activist burnout from regular burnout, noting that it goes beyond occasional bad days or temporary stress. They described activist burnout as "a chronic condition … that results in people once highly committed to a movement or cause or organization growing mentally exhausted, thus losing the idealism and the spirit that once drove them to work for social change" (Chen & Gorski, 2015, p. 368). The research underscores the high risk of burnout among activists, with Klandermans (2003) estimating burnout rates to be as high as 50% to 60%.

Causes

Scholars investigating activist burnout, especially within SJHR activism, propose that activists are particularly susceptible due to their deeply rooted commitments to SJHR causes. Emotional labor, a concept outlined by Goodwin and Pfaff (2001), is central to SJHR activism. SJHR activists invest emotionally in their activism, bearing the self-imposed expectation of making a significant impact (Chen et al., 2024; Pines, 1994). As Pines (1994) pointed out, the root cause of burnout lies in the need to believe that one's life is meaningful, that one's actions are significant and even heroic. Activists, especially those engaged in SJHR causes, are acutely aware of substantial and overwhelming societal problems that others may choose to ignore (Maslach & Gomes, 2006). This unique nature of activist work makes SJHR activists particularly vulnerable to stress, self-imposed pressure, and social isolation (Kovan & Dirkx, 2003).

Additional stressors contributing to activist burnout within the SJHR community include tumultuous relationships within activist organizations. Gomes (1992) documented such stressors within the U.S. peace movement, while Hopgood (2006) found similar tensions in the International Secretariat of Amnesty International. These tensions often arise from differing views within activist organizations, where some advocate for traditional focuses, while others push for more overtly political stances and broader coverage of human rights issues.

Workload and time pressures have also been identified as common stressors (Klandermans, 2003; Vaccaro & Mena, 2011). In addition, the feeling of not being acknowledged and/or valued have been identified as among the factors that contribute to burnout (Nair, 2004).

Research consistently demonstrates that identity profoundly influences well-being among activists. Over the years, studies have underscored the significant toll that cultural, institutional, and individual oppressive forces exert on individuals who identify as marginalized or part of a minoritized group (French et al., 2020; Hope et al., 2018). These oppressive dynamics often erode the resilience of individuals with marginalized identities, rendering them more susceptible to the trauma and adversity. As a result, activists with marginalized identities are more prone to experiencing symptoms of burnout, depression, anxiety, and other mental health issues (Gorski, 2019; Krueger et al., 2022; Vaccaro & Mena, 2011).

For some activists from marginalized communities, the burden of burnout is further intensified. They must challenge the oppressions they face through their activism and contend with those within activist circles (Leondar-Wright, 2014; Lorde, 1988; Plyler, 2006; Wineman, 2003). Additionally, as Gorski and Erakat (2019) indicated, activists with privileged identities can inadvertently heighten the risk of burnout for their marginalized counterparts due to their unevolved or racist views and exhibited White fragility. This often unacknowledged layer of stress exacerbates burnout, highlighting the need for greater sensitivity and support within activist movements to address these pressures.

It should be noted that individuals with intersecting identities engaging in activism face heightened risks and costs (we elaborate on this discussion more deeply in Chapter Three of this volume.) Navigating multiple identities often leads to feelings of exhaustion. When these compounding factors are combined with the pressures of activism, they can result in burnout, post-traumatic stress disorder (PTSD), or suicidal ideation (Vaccaro & Mena, 2011).

Despite the toll that SJHR activism takes, many organizations and groups dismiss discussions or reflections on activist burnout (Pigni, 2013; Plyler, 2006). This lack of acknowledgment, and sometimes even the suppression of concerns about activists' well-being, can accelerate burnout (Nair, 2004). Rodgers (2010) uncovered a culture of selflessness within Amnesty International, where conversations about burnout challenges were rare, and such challenges were seen as sacrifices for the greater cause. Similarly, Chen and Gorski (2015) observed a "culture of martyrdom" or a "guilt culture" that was rooted in an "ethic of suffering" and complete "self-sacrifice." One activist described this stating that: "A lot of activist spaces where people are just killing themselves and don't engage in self-care in very comprehensive ways and don't really think about how to act in measured ways" (Chen & Gorski, 2015, p. 379).

Other potential causes of burnout among SJHR activists, such as power struggles within organizations and movements, have been linked back to this culture of selflessness and the lack of self-care (Nair, 2004; Pigni, 2013; Rodgers, 2010). Plyler (2006) expressed concern that, rather than finding ways to care for themselves and fellow activists, SJHR groups often lose committed members to burnout, leading to fragmentation and a lack of reflection within the movements.

Symptoms

Scholars who have explored activist burnout and activists sharing their firsthand experiences within specific movements or organizations have identified a wide range of defining symptoms (Kovan & Dirkx, 2003; Plyler, 2006; Rettig, 2006). When considering burnout within the SJHR community, Kovan and Dirkx (2003) observed cognitive symptoms among environmental activists, while Vaccaro and Mena (2011) noted physical manifestations of burnout in LGBTQ+ activists of color. Maslach and Gomes (2006) synthesized many of these symptoms into three primary signs of activist burnout, which they discovered among peace activists: (1) exhaustion (feeling emotionally and physically drained), (2) cynicism (developing negative perceptions of once-significant work), and (3) inefficacy (doubting one's self-worth and perceiving a lack of activist accomplishments). They referred to these as the "smoldering embers" that remain when the initial enthusiasm, dedication, and commitment to the cause have faded (Maslach & Gomes, 2006, p. 43). Other researchers have expanded upon these findings. For example, Vaccaro and Mena (2011) complicated prior research by suggesting that their interviewees' lack of self-care was a symptom of their burnout, possibly related to cynicism and inefficacy.

Implications

Scholars and activists who have examined the issue of burnout have made it abundantly clear how detrimental these symptoms can be for individual activists. Burnout stands as a prominent factor influencing whether activists stay engaged or disengage from their activism (Cox, 2009, 2011; Downton & Wehr, 1998; Klandermans, 2003; Pines, 1994). Particularly, those who ignore the signs of burnout and persist in active involvement often find themselves ultimately departing from activism (Gomes & Maslach, 1991). Rettig (2006), for instance, pointed out that "when an activist burns out, she typically derails her career and damages her self-esteem and relationships" (p. 16). This is primarily because activists experiencing burnout often reduce their involvement or completely disengage from their activism (Maslach & Gomes, 2006; Rodgers, 2010; Vaccaro & Mena, 2011). Rettig (2006) even defined burnout as "the act of involuntarily leaving activism or reducing one's level of activism" (p. 16).

What is even more concerning, though, is the adverse effect of activist burnout on SJHR movements. Rettig (2006) lamented that the burned-out activist "also deprives her organization and movement of her valuable experience and wisdom" and concluded: "The worst problem, however, may be that when an activist burns out she deprives younger activists of a mentor, thus making them more likely to burn out" (p. 16).

The impact of burnout on activists extends beyond personal careers and organizational success; it also reverberates throughout the communities or the world that activists serve, adding an additional layer of responsibility and pressure on activists (Kovan & Dirkx, 2003; Pines, 1994). In other words, comprehending the nature of activist burnout and finding ways to alleviate it is not only vital for sustaining the dedication of individual activists but is also an imperative step in maintaining the continuity of social movements (Lorde, 1988; Plyler, 2006; Wollman & Wexler, 1992).

Responding to Activist Burnout

The methods through which activists can manage burnout have attracted scholarly attention. Wollman and Wexler (1992) made early attempts to apply psychology to assist activists, using both didactic and experiential approaches to address this issue. Downton and Wehr (1998), in their examination of 30 peace activists, identified various factors, including forming an activist identity and holding beliefs that emphasize feeling connected to the activist community, as key to sustaining activist commitment. Scholars have also offered several specific individual-level tools to combat the issue. For instance, Maslach and Gomes (2006) suggested that improving health, learning relaxation techniques for challenging situations, and recognizing personal limits may assist activists in coping with burnout.

Effectively addressing the issue of burnout necessitates individual efforts as well as support from communities and organizations (Maslach & Leiter, 2005). For example, Nepstad (2004) found that strategies fostering community building and providing consistent material and emotional support aided participants in the Plowshares movement in overcoming burnout. Maslach and Gomes (2006) recommended that, at the organizational level, accomplishments should be acknowledged, and interpersonal relationships within movements require attention. Others suggested that organizational efforts should focus on providing opportunities for professional growth (Kovan & Dirkx, 2003), fostering peaceful and equitable relationships among activists (Gomes, 1992), and assisting activists in managing stress through exercise and hobbies (Maslach & Leiter, 2005).

Student Activist Burnout

While it is widely understood that student activists also grapple with burnout, academic research in this area is still in its early stages. Vaccaro and Mena (2011), in their phenomenological analysis of queer college activists of color and mental health, discovered that student narratives revealed experiences of "external and internal pressures, limited social support, poor boundaries, and a lack of self-care" (p. 339). Additionally, they noted that students' encounters with intersections between their identities and activism led to experiences of burnout, compassion fatigue, and, in some instances, even thoughts of suicide (Vaccaro & Mena, 2011 p. 339). Broadly echoing this sentiment, Bjornsen-Ramig and Kissinger (2018) explored the mental health of college student activists and observed that, for these students, "the personal is political" (p. 224).

Already marginalized students become further exposed through their advocacy work. In their critical narrative inquiry into student activism as labor, Linder and colleagues (2019) further emphasized the adverse effects of activism on college student activists with minoritized identities. Drawing from conversations with 25 participants, they shared significant findings:

> Student activists with minoritized identities experienced serious emotional, physical, and mental costs associated with activism. Students consistently reported that their relationships and academic pursuits suffered due to their activism, and they described feelings of exhaustion and burnout. (p. 57)

It was concluded that the consequences faced by college student activists as a result of their activist work are substantial and warrant attention from administrators (Linder et al., 2019). Nevertheless, despite these consequences and the urgency of supporting student activists, there is still a significant gap in our understanding of their experiences. We know too little about how their experiences differ (or do not differ) from non-student activists, the impact of burnout on student activists, and potential interventions. Therefore, this chapter aims to illuminate student activists' lived experience, with a particular focus on burnout among this distinct and growing segment within the activist community that requires further investigation.

Findings

Burnout: The Cost of College Student Activism

In this chapter, our attention is drawn to how the 119 college student activists who were interviewed for this study and engaged in SJHR advocacy/activism described their encounters with burnout. Our research confirmed that these students were not immune to the pressures and challenges activism presented. As we explored the connection between SJHR activism and burnout among college student activists, a disheartening revelation emerged: A robust link exists between SJHR activism and burnout among these students.

Participants in our study repeatedly emphasized how their involvement in activism contributed to their burnout. David P., a first-year graduate student dedicated to combating racism through activism, expressed this sentiment, highlighting that burnout or "fatigue [is] the biggest challenge" he faces in his activism work. This experience of burnout was a common thread among the student participants, as 103 (about 87%) of the 119 individuals explicitly acknowledged experiencing some form of burnout or fatigue. Cheryl, a junior and a political organizer, for instance, candidly shared her bout with burnout-induced anxiety, recounting an incident where she "snapped at [her roommate] this morning … It was an anxiety attack. It wasn't full-on. It was just me panicking in my room …trying to collect myself … It just feels so overwhelming."

Through our interactions with the participants, we developed a comprehensive understanding of the root causes of burnout, the apparent "symptoms," and how students responded to these challenges. These findings will be discussed more extensively below.

Burnout Causes: Overextension, Balance Struggles, Institutional Barriers, Activist Work

Overextension. Clara C., another first-year graduate student advocating for immigrant families and children, shared: "Sometimes, I feel like burnout and anxiety go hand in hand. You want to do so much … don't know how or when to stop, or when to take breaks." Clara's observation of not knowing when or how to pause with respect to activism highlighted a potential cause of burnout: Overextension. This sentiment was echoed by Dana, a senior passionate about veterans' issues, who felt burnout stemmed from "Never taking time for me. It's a constant give, give, give." Cheryl shared Dana's observations, emphasizing the collective pressure to keep commitments: "Sometimes, I wish I could just leave for a couple of weeks and get my [sh*t] together, but I really can't. How can I expect people to keep their word if I can't keep mine?" Cheryl further elaborated on the need to be omnipresent:

> I was like, "OK, I'm going to campus, and I have committed to going to the prison labor working group for half an hour," … But then right after that, we are flyering for an hour, and then right after that, we are chalking for an hour, and [one activist] is in Arlington and [another activist] can't do it, so … I have to do those things. I have committed to doing those things. If I'm not there and someone shows up, we're screwed, because then they're not going to come back.

Clara, Dana, and Cheryl, each in their unique way, highlighted the relentless pressure to continue working, advocating, organizing, and marching, regardless of their own needs or limitations. The concept of "overextension," expressed by 94 (about 79%) of the 119 participants, was vividly captured by Clara in her reflection of her responsibilities and obligations:

> I just feel like with jobs and school, it's very easy to get burned out … not only am I working with the kids … you're always going to be dealing with parents as well. That's just more on top, and on top, and on top.

Balance Struggles. Hinted at in Clara's remarks is the difficulty of balancing various responsibilities, a second cause of burnout. Jillian, a junior focusing on reproductive rights and biracial identity, shed light on her struggle with balance: "I try to keep [advocacy] separate from my friend group and … family life. I had a very difficult time … when I first started … It got so exhausting, I burned out." Jillian's comments about the importance of "separateness" are noteworthy because they illuminate how difficulties in achieving balance and overextension contributed to burnout.

George, a 23-year-old White male and first-year graduate student advocating for well-being, revealed how he lost his sense of balance in various aspects of his life, resulting in severe burnout. He explained that he had been concentrating all his energy on his activism work, leading to physical and mental risks for himself:

> I definitely lost my sense of balance in so many ways and really was feeling extremely burnt out. I knew that I could not continue to do that the way that I was doing it where I was focusing all of my attention on that work. It's so easy to not make space for mindfulness and make space for time of reflection and time for self-care … It can feel like that work isn't as important.

Institutional Barriers. The concept of balance among these student activists has drawn attention to the institutional demands required for successful student life. However, these institutions' interactions with students have also emerged as significant sources of burnout due to students' perceived lack of support with respect to their SJHR work as well as the absence of formal training to facilitate such efforts. It was particularly concerning to discover that, at the institutional level, there was a scarcity of structured training or mentorship programs for activists, as only 27 (about 23%) out of the 119 study participants mentioned having received formal training. Others had to seek it through alternative avenues. In addressing the institutional support for student activists, Lawrence, a senior actively engaged in political activism at the time of our interview with him, remarked on the insufficient provision of institution-sanctioned or initiated mentoring related to activism as follows: "Personally, I have not received a lot of training, but I know there are people trying to push that currently. I'm hoping in the next couple of years there will be facilities for that."

Esther, a graduate student specializing in environmental justice, corroborated Lawrence's observation, highlighting how institutional support seemed to be an afterthought. Esther explained that:

> I've recently seen it mentioned, almost as an addendum. It's like, "These are all the things you need to be advocating for, and here's why, blah, blah, blah." But also, don't forget to take care of yourself. It's presented almost as a minor side note.

Susan, a junior at the time of our interview and a student dedicated to transparency in higher education, emphasized the connection between institutional indifference and the arduous nature of her specific form of student activism. Susan revealed: "It's challenging to be an activist at this [school], especially because [administrator name] holds a strong negative stance toward us." Jennifer T., a senior engaged in higher education activism, also commented on institutional support, noting: "Our faculty advisor, I believe for strategic reasons, maintains a somewhat hands-off approach to our work. There's a noticeable level of antagonism from the administration." Karen, a junior working on environmental justice, summarized the sentiments shared by Lawrence, Esther, Susan, and Jennifer:

> It affects some more than others. This … can be very stressful on one's mental health … not healthy. Being introduced to all these ideas and constantly working on them can impact your mental health negatively if you don't have the right tools and the right support system around you.

Activist Work. These considerations of systems and institutions hold particular significance for student activists, as they are, by definition, students bound by university regulations. Consequently, the root causes of burnout identified above, particularly those related to balance and institutional obstacles, may be unique to the experiences of student activists.

In addition, several activists have highlighted the content-heavy nature of their activist work as a significant contributor to their burnout. Amanda, a Latina woman working on sexual violence and women's rights, expressed:

> I would say a lot because it's a very tough issue to keep learning about and to talk about especially because people always ask why

> like, why did you get into it? Why do you want to do this and it's hard because reliving that story, liv[ing] in that memory is very draining. I wouldn't say it was like, you know, sad, but not completely sad, but it's draining you know, so I think fatigue just comes with activism sometimes because it's a heavy subject.

Chrissy, a White woman focusing on graduate and professional student rights, also shared her experience:

> I deal with a really tough subject matter in my research. So obviously, the data that I collect and the interviews that I do, and things like that are very intensive subject matter. It's about abuse. It's about harm, even if people don't qualify it as abuse. It's people telling me narratives of things that have given them a lot of trouble—[it] has given me a lot of stress.

It is noteworthy that some students identified slow progress as leading to their burnout. Benjamin, identifying as non-binary and White working on LGBTQ+ rights and politics and policy, elaborated:

> For me, I just get irritable. When I'm tired, when things aren't going my way, when change, again is slow, is not happening in what I would think is an efficient and effective pace. I get irritable, I get angry, I get short, I get hurt.

And, Bob, a White man focusing on education, echoed the following:

> There have been times I felt that no changes will be made locally, statewide, nationally, or even institutionally at … things that I see as glaring problems. When I get in this mindset, I become hopeless, void of energy physically and mentally, depressed, and anxious. This has caused me immense stress regarding both the present and future of our country and world.

Burnout Symptoms: Physical and Mental Manifestations

Our study reveals a strong link between burnout and physical symptoms. This connection between burnout and physical well-being, along with potential mental health concerns, was acknowledged by Karen. When reflecting on her activist work and its potential connection to PTSD, Karen described her experience of burnout as occurring "in waves." She expressed: "I experience it most when something unexpected comes along and there has to be an immediate action … That just gives me … a lot of anxiety to have to be really quick to come to that."

Anxiety emerged as a prominent symptom among 75 (63%) of the 119 participants. Cheryl detailed her experiences with burnout-induced anxiety, recounting an incident where she snapped at her roommate during breakfast and experienced a panic attack, as mentioned earlier.

Esther, when asked to describe the symptoms associated with burnout, also mentioned anxiety. She explained that during a period about a year ago, she began to experience anxiety and panic attacks. Esther attributed these symptoms to the realization that there are numerous issues to address, yet one can only have an impact on a limited number of them. She shared:

> That is a very hard question. I would say that's what I started to describe a minute ago where … I don't know exactly when this would have been, maybe last year sometime, when I had many issues with anxiety and panic attacks were starting, was realizing that you learn about all these issues that are happening, and you can only have an impact on so much.

In addition to anxiety and panic, 59 (49%) of the participants also shared their experiences of depression, guilt, hopelessness, and grief. Dana, reflecting on her activist work, expressed a sense of grief for her cause and feelings of great sadness: "I cry, sometimes. It's like, the grief, and you cry about whatever … just being tired, and everybody's cranky." She mentioned crying and feeling unworthy, describing burnout as a sense of not being heard and not feeling important: "The burnout for me is nobody's hearing me. I'm nobody important … They don't value my opinion as much as somebody in a higher position … soul fatigue."

Eugene, a White man dedicated to fighting gun violence and advocating for LGBTQ+ rights, openly discussed his battle with depression, which he partly attributed to his involvement in activism. He described feelings of hopelessness, the desire to give up, and emotional turmoil when thinking about the impact of societal issues on his family and others. He also expressed guilt:

> I would say I feel hopeless sometimes. I want to give up. I'll stay up crying, because I'll be thinking about how my family's been affected by these issues. I'll think about how other families have been affected by these issues. I feel guilty.

From a physical standpoint, David P. corroborated the accounts of others by affirming the physical toll of student activism. He described burnout as feeling like exhaustion, primarily a mental sensation but one that can manifest as physical fatigue. He noted:

> It feels like exhaustion. It is mostly mental, but it manifests as if it is physical, especially, if I am not setting aside time to re-energize and reinvigorate, I will find myself as if I am physically exhausted, spending a lot of time lounging and almost ignoring the weight of the issues that I'm trying to battle against.

Responses to Burnout: Withdrawal, Coping Strategies, and Self-Care Practices

Through our interviews, it became evident that the students recognized the importance of self-care in addressing activist burnout. Nevertheless, they also acknowledged the challenges in implementing self-care practices. In the absence of self-care, students discussed strategies such as withdrawal from activism or compartmentalization of their activist work.

Past research has shown that withdrawal from social interactions is a typical response to burnout (Maslach & Pines, 1977). Similarly, many participants in this study expressed a need or inclination to disengage from activism when experiencing burnout. At least half of the participants who had experienced burnout explicitly mentioned their consideration of stepping back from activist work. For instance, when asked if he had contemplated "stepping back" due to burnout, Lawrence acknowledged the thought and emphasized the importance of staying connected to one's purpose:

> Oh, definitely. I think everyone has that period of, "I could just quit. I could just step back and stop it," and be like, "I'm done. I'm not a member anymore," but … You have to keep your eye on why you're doing this.

Eugene shared a similar sentiment, acknowledging that passionate activists may experience such thoughts during their journey. Jillian also discussed the value of temporarily removing herself from activism, even if just for a brief period. David offered a different perspective, emphasizing the practice of compartmentalization as a coping mechanism:

> I have [a] pretty strong separation between the activities that I really like to do with my friends in any outdoor community … things of that nature that feel very far-removed from the issues of systemic racism that I work with.

Cheryl echoed David's sentiments, highlighting the importance of spending time with individuals outside of activist circles as a refreshing reminder that activism is not the entirety of one's world. It is worth noting that despite these inclinations toward withdrawal, 111 (93%) of the participants had established some form of self-care practice to combat the adverse effects of burnout. Even without formal training or mentoring, participants reported discovering fulfilling activities, seeking advice from parents and friends, and consulting professional therapists to develop self-care routines.

Self-care practices varied among participants and included activities like the soothing baths preferred by Cheryl, lively dance parties favored by Hannah R., outdoor adventures cherished by David, and gym sessions embraced by Illio. Karen encapsulated the collective sentiment:

> The thing is … you can't be fighting constantly. There's a time when your arms grow tired, and you just can't swing anymore. You have to learn how to go back into the corner, take a few deep breaths and come out again, and keep sustaining the fight … . we can pull back, reflect, take care of ourselves. When we do that, we make our movement stronger.

Considering the "culture of martyrdom" present in the activist communities (Chen & Gorski, 2015), we also explored issues of privilege surrounding self-care. When asked if they regarded self-care as a luxury, 30 (about 25%) of the participants acknowledged that it could be seen as a privilege but emphasized its necessity for the effectiveness of their work. Hannah aptly summarized this viewpoint:

> It absolutely is a place of privilege to be able to find self-care or self-care practices. A lot of people don't have that same access to find those, or don't have the same access to people in their life that are going to tell them, "Hey, take some time for yourself," and things like that.

Karen concurred with Hannah, acknowledging that while self-care might be considered a luxury, neglecting it would diminish the impact of their activism: "it is a luxury to have time. At the same time, if you don't take at least a little bit of time for yourself … the efforts you put into your movement are … not going to be as impactful." In contrast, Illio, a first-year student passionate about various issues, believed that self-care should be a top priority for everyone and not a privilege: "I have always thought that self-care should be at the top of everyone's own personal list because you can't do all the things … you want to do unless you take care of yourself first."

These narratives highlight the need to distinguish between two broad kinds of privileges: The types that everyone deserves, which ought to be considered natural, like access to safe housing and clean water, compared with the privilege—or as Ross Gay (2022) calls it, "disprivilege"—that bestows unfair advantages on some and gives those same people the right to oppress others, what McIntosh (2015) calls "conferred advantage." Hannah's reflection underscores the idea that self-care can be seen as a privilege, given that not everyone has equal access to the necessary resources and support. This aligns with the notion of "conferred advantage." Conversely, Illio's perspective emphasizes that self-care should be universally prioritized, challenging the idea that it is an exclusive privilege and suggesting that it should be considered "natural."

To sum up, our research has unveiled significant insights regarding college student activists. The study affirmed the presence of burnout as a prominent concern among student activists, with causes rooted in factors like overextension, challenges in balancing commitments, and institutional obstacles. We also examined the physical and mental health consequences of burnout experienced by these students, as manifested through their reported symptoms. Finally, we explored how students cope with burnout by either withdrawing from activism, compartmentalizing their involvement, or embracing self-care practices. In the discussion section below, we will endeavor to analyze the implications and meaning of these findings for practice.

Discussion and Implications for Research and Practice

Our study has unearthed crucial distinctions between student activist burnout and those experienced by non-student activists. These disparities primarily stem from the unique "student" context, characterized by juggling academic, personal, and activist commitments, and the complex power dynamics within institutional systems, which influence both the causes of and responses to burnout.

Corinne Ruff (2016) highlighted the struggle of student activists in balancing coursework and advocacy, which resonates with our findings that the difficulty of balancing activism, academics, and personal life is a significant cause of burnout for student activists. This dual role as students and activists presents a notable challenge, and our participants revealed that navigating this terrain has been a learning process, leading to periodic struggles in fulfilling both roles effectively.

Another distinguishing aspect is the institutional framework within which student activists operate. Navigating this system as students, while simultaneously pursuing their activism, can be particularly challenging. This institutional dimension adds an extra layer of burden and potential burnout triggers, particularly for minority student activists facing institutional oppression or institutional betrayal (Linder et al., 2019). See Chapter Five of this volume for more on the effects of institutions of higher education on student activist well-being (Table 4.2).

Our findings suggest that student activists experience significant unpleasant emotions due to their activism work. These unpleasant emotions, such as sadness, anger, and stress, directly impact their subjective well-being. For instance, the constant need to balance

Table 4.2 Subjective Well-being Components and Sample Sub-components

Pleasant Emotions	*Unpleasant Emotions*	*Life Judgments*	*Domain Satisfaction*
Joy	Sadness	Life satisfaction	Marriage
Contentment	Anger	Fulfillment	Work
Happiness	Worry	Meaning	Health
Love	Stress	Success	Leisure

Note: Adapted from Diener and colleagues (2009).

academic responsibilities with activist efforts can lead to increased stress and worry, negatively affecting their SWB outlined by Diener and colleagues (2009).

In terms of responses to burnout, student activists share similarities with their non-student counterparts, such as reducing their level of activism (Chen & Gorski, 2015). Our study, however, suggests that student activists are more aware of the issue of burnout compared with non-student activists, who often view burnout as a "taboo" topic due to a prevailing "culture of martyrdom" (Gorski & Chen, 2015). There appears to be a generational gap in discussing activist burnout, with younger activists more comfortable addressing mental health issues, likely due to increased media and online discussions fostering empathy, as suggested by some of our participants like Eugene.

Regrettably, student activists and non-student activists alike receive minimal institutional or formal training, mentoring, or coaching to proactively cope with burnout (Chen & Gorski, 2015). With these findings in mind, we must focus on intervention, practice, and further research. Scholars have proposed various individual-level strategies to help SJHR activists manage burnout, such as enhancing self-esteem, recognizing personal needs, and maintaining a balance between self-care and activism. Jacob and colleagues (2009) have also suggested the potential benefits of meditative and mindful practices in promoting activists' well-being. Additionally, interventions like ecological drama therapy, as Hart (2013) demonstrated, can offer valuable insights into self-care strategies.

Nevertheless, addressing student activist burnout requires attention at the individual level and within the broader community and institutional context (Rhoads, 2009). Universities should implement formal training policies to equip student activists with tools to manage burnout. Resources like the Human Rights Resilience Project's website (available at www.hrresilience.org/) offer valuable support models. Recognizing that student activist burnout affects both activists and the communities they serve, institutions must prioritize this issue.

Lastly, further research should dig deeper into understanding the unique needs of student activists. This includes exploring how student activists differ from their non-student counterparts in responding to systemic pressures and institutional challenges. Scholars should also examine the specific risks and rewards associated with student activism within a university setting, encompassing factors like academic performance, family distance, burnout, leadership development, community building, and a sense of belonging.

Conclusion

While we acknowledge that the activist experience is multifaceted (Conner, 2020), burnout looms large among student activists. As reflected in the scant scholarship on this issue, the limited attention to student activist burnout within SJHR discourses and practices has detrimental consequences for both the activists themselves and the societies where they engage in their work, particularly marginalized communities.

Student activists are unique in their dual roles as students, and it is imperative that post-secondary institutions prioritize their well-being. Universities must develop corresponding intervention tools and policies to address student activist burnout. The passion for positive social change and the pressures and pitfalls of activism are inseparable for student activists. As educators committed to holistic student development, we must align with the higher education mission of nurturing engaged citizens and acknowledge the labor and outcomes of student activism.

Scholarship in Action
Burnout and College Student Activism

Thought Questions:

For students: How would you balance your academic responsibilities with activism, and what strategies do you think are most effective to prevent burnout?

Reflect on a time when you felt overwhelmed by your roles as both a student and an activist/advocate/ally. What specific factors contributed to these feelings?

For staff/practitioners: What initiatives could be implemented at universities to better support student activists? How can staff contribute to a culture that recognizes and mitigates the risks of burnout among student activists?

For faculty: In what ways can curriculum development include discussions about the dual challenges faced by student activists? How can faculty members use their positions to advocate for institutional changes that support student activists?

For community partners: How can community organizations that work with student activists ensure these students are supported and not overextended? What roles can community partners play in recognizing and alleviating burnout in student activists?

For researchers: What gaps exist in the current research on burnout among student activists, and how can future studies address these gaps? How can research findings be effectively communicated to policymakers to influence change in how institutions support student activists?

Resources for Additional Learning:

Websites:

This resource provides information and tools for student mental health, including sections on activism.
www.hrresilience.org/resources.html

This resource focuses on supporting the mental health and emotional well-being of young people of color who are often engaged in activism.
https://wellbeing.gmu.edu/research/thriving-activist-toolkit/

Training and Certifications:

Mental Health First Aid: www.mentalhealthfirstaid.org
Training on how to assist someone experiencing a mental health-related crisis.

Books:

Obear, K. (2018). *In it for the long haul: Overcoming burnout and passion fatigue as social justice change agents.* Morgan James Publishing.

In this volume, Obear shares her own journey with burnout and passion fatigue, and teaches other change agents how to recognize the warning signs of burnout. Through engaging stories and practical tips, the author encourages change agents to recommit to self-care so they can be of greater service and spark real change in the world.

Rettig, H. (2006). *The lifelong activist: How to change the world without losing your way*. Lantern Books.

This book is a guide to living a joyful and productive life, while also minimizing fear, guilt and shame. Clear instructions are offered for how to manage your mission, your time, your fears, and your relationships. Anyone at risk for burnout will find it particularly useful.

Classroom Activities:

Role-Playing Workshops: Students assume roles as student activists, university administrators, and community members to navigate a scenario involving activism and burnout.

Journaling Exercise: Students keep a weekly journal documenting their experiences and reflections on balancing activism with their academic and personal lives.

References

American College Health Association (ACHA). (2018). *National college health assessment II*. ACHA. www.acha.org/NCHA/ACHA-NCHA_Data/Publications_and_Reports/NCHA/Data/Reports_ACHA-NCHAIIc.aspx.

Bjornsen-Ramig, A., & Kissinger, D. (2018). Activism and college student mental health. In M. Miller (Ed.), *Exploring the technological, societal, and institutional dimensions of college student activism* (pp. 217–237). IGI Global.

Chen, C. W., & Gorski, P. C. (2015). Burnout in social justice and human rights activists: Symptoms, causes and implications. *Journal of Human Rights Practice*, *7*(3), 366–390.

Chen, C. W., McCarron, G. P., & Owen, J. E. (2024). The emotional labor of college student activism: An interview-based study. *Journal of Human Rights Practice*. Online First. https://doi.org/10.1093/jhuman/huae025

Conner, J. O. (2020). *The new student activists: The rise of neoactivism on college campuses*. Johns Hopkins University Press.

Conner, J. O., Crawford, E., & Galioto, M. (2023). The mental health effects of student activism: Persisting despite psychological costs. *Journal of Adolescent Research*, *38*(1), 80–109. https://doi.org/10.1177/07435584211006789

Cox, L. (2009). "Hearts with one purpose alone"? Thinking personal sustainability in social movements. *Emotion, Space and Society*, *2*, 52–61. https://eprints.nuim.ie/1538/1/LCHearts_with_one_purpose_alone_LBedited.pdf

Cox, L. (2011). How do we keep going? Activist burnout and personal sustainability in social movements. https://eprints.nuim.ie/2815/1/LC_How_do_we_keep_going.pdf

Diener, E., Scollon, C. N., & Lucas, R. E. (2009). The evolving concept of subjective well-being: The multifaceted nature of happiness. In E. Diener (Ed.), *Assessing well-being: The collected works of Ed Diener* (pp. 67–100). Springer. https://doi.org/10.1007/978-90-481-2354-4

Downton, J., & Wehr, P. (1998). Persistent pacifism: How activist commitment is developed and sustained. *Journal of Peace Research*, *35*(5), 531–550. https://doi.org/10.1177/0022343398035005001

French, B., Lewis, J., Mosley, D., Adames, H., Chaves-Duenas, N., Chen, G., & Neville, H. (2020). Toward a psychological framework of radical healing in communities of color. *The Counseling Psychologist*, *48*(1), 14–46. https://doi.org/10.1177/0011000019843506

Freudenberger, H. J. (1974). Staff burnout. *Journal of Social Issues*, *30*, 159–165.

Gay, R. (2022). *Inciting joy: Essays*. Hodder & Stoughton.

Gomes, M. E. (1992). The rewards and stresses of social change: A qualitative study of peace activists. *Journal of Humanistic Psychology*, *32*(4), 138–146. https://doi.org/10.1177/0022167892324008

Gomes, M. E., & Maslach, C. (1991). Commitment and burnout among political activists: An in-depth study. Paper presented at the International Society of Political Psychology, Helsinki, Finland.

Goodwin, J., & Pfaff, S. (2001). Emotion work in high-risk social movements: Managing fear in the U.S. and East German civil rights movements. In J. Goodwin, J. Jasper, & F. Polletta (Eds.), *Passionate politics: Emotions and social movements* (pp. 282–302). University of Chicago Press.

Gorski, P. C. (2019). Fighting racism, battling burnout: Causes of activist burnout in U.S. racial justice activist. *Ethnic and Racial Studies*, *42*(5), 667–687. https://doi.org/10.1080/01419870.2018.1439981

Gorski, P. C., & Chen, C. W. (2015). "Frayed all over:" The causes and consequences of activist burnout among social justice education activists. *Educational Studies*, *51*(5), 385–405. https://doi.org/10.1080/00131946.2015.1075989

Gorski, P. C., & Erakat, N. (2019). Racism, whiteness, and burnout in anti-racism movements: How white racial justice activists elevate burnout in racial justice activists of color in the United States. *Ethnicities*, *19*(5), 784–808. https://doi.org/10.1177/1468796819833871

Hart, R. (2013). *Widening circles of care: Exploring self-care with activists using ecological drama therapy* [Unpublished master's thesis, Concordia University].

Hartson, K. R., Hall, L. A., & Choate, S. A. (2023). Stressors and resilience are associated with well-being in young adult college students. *Journal of American College Health*, *71*(3), 821–829. https://doi.org/10.1080/07448481.2021.1908309

Hope, E., Velez, G., Offidani Bertrand, C., Keels, M., & Durkee, M. I. (2018). Political activism and mental health among Black and Latinx college students. *Cultural Diversity and Ethnic Minority Psychology*, *24(*1), 26–39. https://doi.org/10.1037/cdp0000144

Hopgood, S. (2006). *Keepers of the flame: Understanding Amnesty International*. Cornell University Press.

Jacob, J., Jovic, E., & Brinkerhoff, M. B. (2009). Personal and planetary well-being: Mindfulness meditation, pro-environmental behavior and personal quality of life in a survey from the social justice and ecological sustainability movement. *Social Indicators Research*, *93*(2), 275–294. https://doi.org/10.1007/s11205-008-9308-6

Klandermans, B. (2003). Collective political action. In D. O. Sears, L. Huddy, & R. Jervis (Eds.), *Oxford handbook of political psychology* (pp. 670–709). Oxford University Press.

Kovan, J. T., & Dirkx, J. M. (2003). "Being called awake:" The role of transformative learning in the lives of environmental activists. *Adult Education Quarterly*, *53*(2), 99–118. https://doi.org/10.1177/0741713602238906

Krueger, N. T., Garba, R., Stone-Sabali, S., Cokley, K. O., & Bailey, M. (2022). African American activism: The predictive role of race related stress, racial identity, and social justice beliefs. *Journal of Black Psychology*, *48*(3-4), 273–308. https://doi.org/10.1177/0095798420984660

Leondar-Wright, B. (2014). *Missing Class: Strengthening social movement groups by seeing class cultures* (1st Ed.). Cornell University Press. https://doi.org/10.7591/9780801470714

Linder, C., Quaye, S. J., Lange, A. C., Roberts, R. E., Lacy, M. C., & Okello, W. K. (2019). "A student should have the privilege of just being a student:" Student activism as labor. *The Review of Higher Education*, *42*(5), 37–62. https://doi.org/10.1353/rhe.2019.0044

Lorde, A. (1988). *A burst of light: And other essays*. Ixia Press.

Maslach, C., & Gomes, M. E. (2006). Overcoming burnout. In R. M. MacNair (Ed.), *Working for peace: A handbook of practical psychology* (2nd Ed., pp. 43–49). Impact Publishers.

Maslach, C., & Leiter, M. P. (2005). Reversing burnout: How to rekindle your passion for your work. *Stanford Social Innovation Review*, *3*(4), 42–49. https://doi.org/10.1109/EMR.2010.5645760

Maslach, C., & Pines, A. (1977). The burnout syndrome in the day care setting. *Child Care Quarterly*, *6*, 100–113.

McIntosh, P. (2015). Extending the knapsack: Using the white privilege analysis to examine conferred advantage and disadvantage. *Women & Therapy*, *38*(3–4), 232–245. https://doi.org/10.1080/02703149.2015.1059195

Nair, N. (2004). On "being" and "becoming:" The many faces of an activist. *Agenda*, *60*, 28–32.

Nepstad, S. E. (2004). Persistent resistance: Commitment and community in the Plowshares movement. *Social Problems*, *51*(1), 43–60. https://doi.org/10.1525/sp.2004.51.1.43

Pigni, A. (2013). Practising mindfulness at the checkpoint. In *Open Democracy (London)*. OpenDemocracy.

Pines, A. M. (1994). Burnout in political activism: An existential perspective. *Journal of Health and Human Resources Administration*, *16*(4), 381–394.

Plyler, J. (2006). How to keep on keeping on. *Upping the Anti*, *3*, 123–134.

Rettig, H. (2006). *The lifelong activist: How to change the world without losing your way*. Lantern Books. https://lifelongactivist.com

Rhoads, R. (2009). Learning from students as agents of social change: Toward an emancipatory vision of the university. *Journal of Change Management*, *9*(3), 309–322. https://doi.org/10.1080/14697010903125555

Rodgers, K. (2010). "Anger is why we're all here:" Mobilizing and managing emotions in a professional activist organization. *Social Movement Studies*, *9*(3), 273–291. https://doi.org/10.1080/14742837.2010.493660

Ruff, C. (2016, March 16). The mental and academic costs of campus activism. *The Chronicle of Higher Education*. www.chronicle.com/article/The-MentalAcademic-Costs/235711

Schaufeli, W. B., & Buunk. P. (2002). Burnout: An overview of 25 years of research and theorizing. In M. J. Schabracq, J. A. M. Winnubst, & C. L. Cooper (Eds.), *The handbook of work and health psychology* (pp. 383–425). Wiley.

Vaccaro, A., & Mena, J. (2011). It's not burnout, it's more: Queer college activists of color and mental health. *Journal of Gay and Lesbian Mental Health*, *15*(4), 339–367. https://doi.org/10.1080/19359705.2011.600656

Wineman, S. (2003). *Power-under: Trauma and non-violent social change*. Author.

Wollman, N., & Wexler, M. (1992). A workshop for activists: Giving psychology away to peace and justice workers. *Journal of Humanistic Psychology*, *32*(4), 147–156. https://doi.org/10.1177/0022167892324009

5 Community

Bridging Self and Collective Care

> *It can get really frustrating when you're trying to promote a cause, support change, and nothing is happening. For example, trying to get the name changed on several buildings on campus. Several [student] organizations have been working for years trying to get these buildings renamed ... . This is really frustrating because you put in all this work and you want to see a change and it's just not happening and [you are] not getting any sort of support from people and places of power ... . it can get really discouraging and you kind of start to lose hope, I guess. But then, when you're talking with your members and getting support from your community that can be a little extra energetic boost that gets you to keep going. That is just part of activism, you face obstacles, but you have to pick yourself up, dust yourself off and keep going.* —Naomi

Naomi, a White woman student whose activism focuses on issues of reproductive rights, women's rights, and LGBTQ+ rights, discussed the challenges of students trying to make change on campus and the revitalizing power of a supportive community. These themes of the importance of community as a bridge between self and collective care echoed across many of our interviews.

Introduction

This chapter addresses the personal, pedagogical, and institutional structures of on- and off-campus communities that empower and constrain student activist well-being. Rather than merely being supportive or limiting, each of these types of communities offers a complex mix of forces that can both hinder and bolster student activist

DOI: 10.4324/9781003481010-5

well-being. First, this chapter examines the roles of activist communities beyond campuses and how these communities may shape student activists' identity, sense of belonging, understanding of social issues, and overall well-being. Activist communities can function as an important bridge between self-care and collective care. Next, institutions of higher education themselves are considered as sites of activism and community engagement. College student activism both shapes, and is shaped by, campus environments, context, and culture. The literature review concludes with a look at how individual educators and administrators can affect student activists' well-being through policies, programs, and pedagogies. Findings from our research study are presented, with special emphasis on how participants navigated both activist and campus communities, and the perceived effects of these environments and educators on their well-being. Viewing institutions of higher education as community partners could allow for enhanced reciprocity and student well-being. Recommendations for research and practice are offered for educators, activists, and educational institutions.

Literature Review

Activist Communities and Well-Being

Activist communities are an important part of shaping student activists' identity, sense of belonging, understanding of social issues, and overall well-being. Chapter Three in this volume details the roles of identity and activism. Being part of a community of activists, whether on- or off-campus, can also be considered a form of student engagement, a type of civic involvement, and a pathway for leadership (Grim et al., 2019; Linder, 2019; Renn, 2007). Activist communities can amplify students' sense of belonging and even their access to information related to social issues and causes (Linder et al., 2019b). Perhaps most importantly, activist communities can play a pivotal role in student well-being (Chen & Gorski, 2015).

Prior research on activism has highlighted the role various communities play in supporting or hindering student activist well-being (Chen & Gorski, 2015; Miller & Tolliver, 2017; Rhoads, 1998b). In their study of burnout in social justice advocates, Gorski and Chen (2015) found three symptom categories of activist burnout including the deterioration of psychological and emotional well-being, the deterioration of physical well-being, and disillusionment and hopelessness. While each of these symptoms can be exacerbated by activist communities, they can also be ameliorated by being in community. For example, the presence of a "culture of martyrdom" within social justice activist communities and organizations, can lead activists to consider self-care as self-indulgence, and to feel guilty if they take steps to address their own well-being (Gorski & Chen, 2015; Rodgers, 2010). Conversely, activist communities can also provide support and resources about how to guard against activist burnout, and provide social, emotional, and practical reciprocity, which builds stress resistance (Ozbay et al., 2007).

Some activist communities do little to discuss or to develop resources for coping with activist burnout, which can lead members to withdraw from activism. Additionally, there may be strained relationships and tensions within an activist organization that contribute to a lack of well-being (Chen & Gorski, 2015; Gomes, 1992; Hopgood, 2006). In their study of burnout in social justice and human rights activists, Chen and Gorski (2015) found that aside from one participant, no respondents reported receiving any "mentoring on coping with burnout or opportunities to have open, honest conversations about burnout" (p. 378). In a study of Amnesty International organizations, Hopgood (2006) found deep tensions between community members who had different visions for the organization—for example, there was conflict about how many overtly political stances the organization should adopt as it works to address human rights issues. Other activists describe community infighting about who receives grants or credit for the work (Chen & Gorski, 2015). The costs of activist communities ignoring member well-being are legion. In addition to deleterious effects on members' physical and emotional health, there can also be motivation manifestations (Schaufeli & Buunk, 2002) resulting in diminished commitment and even withdrawal from activist organizations and causes. Chen and Gorski (2015) underscored the larger implications of activist flight from causes and communities, in that it may mean fewer people working to address injustice and human rights abuses.

Conversely, activist communities can also support activist well-being by embedding self-care into organizational conversations and programs. Chen and Gorski (2015) review actions activist communities can take to support the well-being of their members. Organizations should take care to foster healthy within-movement interpersonal relations, as well as to acknowledge individual member contributions and overall movement accomplishments (Maslach & Gomes, 2006). Activist communities can also promote activities related to coping with stress such as exercise and hobbies (Maslach & Leiter, 2005), or to help members link their activist skills with personal and professional growth opportunities (Kovan & Dirkx, 2003). Ozbay and colleagues (2007) showed how social and emotional support, along with reciprocity, can neurologically build stress resistance and resilience. Activist communities that embrace Audre Lorde's (1988) view of self-care as "an act of political warfare" (p. 131), can position individual well-being as central to organizational sustainability and collective well-being (Gorski & Chen, 2015). In this way, activist communities that promote self-care are also engaging in collective care and building both individual and organizational endurance for sustained engagement.

Institutions of Higher Education as Sites of Activism

Student activists, in addition to their activist organizations and larger communities, are also embedded in institutions of higher education such as colleges and universities. There is a strong body of extant research on the relationship between student activists and colleges themselves (Broadhurst & Martin, 2014; Chen et al., 2024; Linder et al., 2019a; McCarron et al., 2023, 2024; Quaye et al., 2021; Rhoads, 1998b; Tolliver et al., 2018). Quaye and colleagues (2021) suggested that college student activism is inherently informed and framed by the institutions where students conduct activism. They note: "campus contexts and environments are salient to the genesis and outcomes of activist movements in that their conditions can either facilitate activism, suppress activism, or both" (Quaye et al., 2021, p. 110). There is no typical U.S. university. Rather, the United States has the most diverse set of higher education institutions in the world resulting in wide-ranging approaches to activism (Quaye et al., 2021).

Quaye and colleagues (2021) also noted that "the institutional factors that can influence activism vary greatly" (p. 111). For example, in a study of student activism related to the #ITooAm social media campaign about racism on campuses, Baker and Blissett (2018) found the following factors as positively predictive of student activism: higher selectivity, larger institutional size, and fewer students receiving Pell

Grants (i.e., fewer students from low-income backgrounds). Socio-historically, some attribute the fact that colleges have been hotbeds of activism to students having time and leisure to focus on social issues, yet that is no longer true for many college students holding multiple jobs and struggling with debt. Conner (2020) posited an alternative view and suggested "we need to know more about how young people negotiate their identities as activists and their relationships with their universities" (p. 3). Why are some students moved to action on political and social issues during the college years, while others remain apolitical and even apathetic? Conner describes this "neoactivism" on campuses, stating:

> Today's youth activists may be just as sanguine about their ability to effect change, but they have come of age in a very different sociopolitical and economic context. … they are responding to a set of conditions that are necessarily different from those faced by previous generations of students. While some of their struggles represent the unfinished work of earlier eras, the new student activists also combat emergent existential crises, like climate change, as well as the by-products of decades of neoliberal policy, such as skyrocketing tuition prices at public universities.
>
> (p. 4)

Communities and Contexts

Activist well-being is shaped by many aspects of higher education communities and contexts. Conner (2020) argued that "to understand the turn toward activism, one must view the student activist and the higher education institution as existing in a dialectical relationship, wherein each challenges the other" (pp. 20–21). Students may arrive on campus with prior activist experiences, and seek to develop a more refined or committed activist identity on campus, which they may "train on the social institution most proximate to them, the university or college" (Conner, 2020, p. 21). Universities are faced with several choices in addressing student concerns and activist efforts. They may listen to and address student concerns (either by placating or enacting change), may defend and maintain the status quo, or may ignore students completely (Conner, 2020; Ropers-Huilman et al., 2005). Does the university become stronger in this dialogic process? Conner (2020) thinks so, stating that "the transformative capacity of the university to impact individuals as well as society hinges on the institution's engagement with student activists" (p. 24).

As for the institution's effects on its students, Barnhardt and colleagues (2015) conducted a mixed-method analysis of college students' civic commitments and capacities for community action. Quantitative findings indicated that, after controlling for background characteristics, campus contexts, and college experiences, students' acquisitions of commitments to and skills for contributing to the larger community are largely influenced by the extent to which students perceive their campus as one that advocates for its students to be active and involved citizens. Other research has indicated that progressive student activists at religiously affiliated private institutions have reported a stifling environment that hampers their efforts (Binder & Kidder, 2022; Chen et al., 2024). In his review of 40 years of student activism on college campuses, Rhoads (1998a) reminds us that "it is reasonable to expect that many of the social tensions of the democratic adventure will be apparent in campus life" (p. 23), and suggests that "student activism [on campus] is not to be taken as a sign that the university is in agony, but instead may be seen as an example of a plurality of voices struggling to be heard" (p. 27).

University Policies, Programs, and Pedagogies

Beyond institutional characteristics, other studies have examined how institutional actors, decision-makers, and leaders shape activist tactics and activities through the creation of policies, programs, and pedagogies (Barnett et al., 2008). Myriad university policies and procedures can be perceived as both supporting and protecting students, as well as potentially limiting and silencing their agency. Quaye and colleagues (2021) describe this interplay as follows:

> The choices administrators, faculty, and staff make inform the context that students maneuver. Policy decisions, connections to local and state legislatures, and (un)willingness to engage in risk shape the context through which students understand institutional leaders as deeply connected to the institution and as representatives of institutional values and action.
>
> (p. 114)

Indeed, while mitigative change efforts are often found in abundance at colleges and universities, institutions of higher education often go to great lengths to avoid truly transformative change. Conner (2020) explains why in the following passage:

> Change is expensive, often involving political and financial costs … institutions of higher education are not in the habit of capitulating to student demands for deep structural change. Though there are examples of student successes, it is often easier for universities to wait them out. Two or four years is not long to wait for activists to exit the system.
>
> (p. 21)

Though the neoliberal university may view students as "purchasers, products, or future sources of funding" (Conner, 2020, p. 22), most student activists view themselves as "critical stakeholders in an institution that stands to serve a vital function in a pluralistic democracy" (p. 22). Students might "renounce the neoliberal university's anemic understanding of its role as a workforce supplier"—they may "call out the neoliberal university's enmeshment in histories of colonialism and racism" and instead offer up an alternative vision of the universities as a civic actor (Conner, 2020, p. 22).

What kinds of tactics are employed in activism at institutions of higher education? Kezar and colleagues' (2011) research examined grassroots leadership tactics used by university administrators, and found tactics varied across organizational contexts. Ropers-Huilman and colleagues (2005) described a range of administrative responses to student activists—from gatekeepers, antagonists, absentee leaders, to supporters. On the supportive side, several studies (Kezar et al., 2011; Linder, 2019) suggested that "the ways faculty and staff contributed to institutional change connected to student activism, including leveraging curricula and classrooms to engage in activist praxis and discussion, mentoring students, hiring people committed to social justice, and partnering with key stakeholders" (Quaye et al., 2021, p. 115). Additional support for student activists includes faculty's own research on activism and their commitments to particular academic departments (Byrd et al., 2019).

Students' campus activism is often responsive to the tone and receptiveness they receive from campus administrators (Broadhurst & Martin, 2014). Research by Barnett and colleagues (2008) found that students are "more likely to use positive strategies in their initial interactions with administrators, and use negative strategies as a last resort" (p. 344). Strategies examined included rational persuasion through the use of facts and logic, coalition-building, and direct pressure such as demands, threats and intimidation. Quaye and colleagues (2021) reframed these results, stating "the more institutional leaders resist student activists, the more activists will use disruptive tactics in their activism" (p. 113). The authors go on to point out that more disruptive activist strategies are not necessarily negative, and can actually be a valuable form of feedback about how to improve campus environments and policies.

Campus Educators and Student Activist Well-Being

In their meta-analysis of scholarship on college student activism from 2000 to 2020, Quaye and colleagues (2021) found that most discussions of higher education "institutions" were in fact focused on the people, communities, and characteristics that comprise institutions, such as institutional leaders, organizational climate and culture, and their effects on student activists. Indeed, communities are composed of individual actors. Apart from campus environments and institutional policies and actions, it is important to consider how individual campus educators might shape student activist well-being. Campus educators can include a wide variety of faculty, staff, and administrators who engage with college students on campus, in and out of the classroom.

Even though many students arrive on campus with prior activist experiences, college students are still "challenged and changed through their coursework and interactions with faculty, staff, and peers" (Conner, 2020, p. 21). Interactions with campus educators are pivotal to student activists' sense of social and emotional support, and to their overall sense of well-being (McCarron et al., 2024). For example, students typically desire to have more access and engagement with university administrators in order to work together to address social issues. However, once participants meet with a lack of response, or a mitigative response from administrators, the relationship between activists and administrators can become more adversarial (McCarron et al., 2024). Additionally, Quaye and colleagues (2021) found that "the social identities of administrators tasked with responding to activists matter when considering how and why staff and administrators engage student activists" (p. 115). Students may feel more attached to educators who share their experiences and identities (Chávez & Ramrakhiani, 2021). Especially related to racial and diversity activism, staff who were once student activists themselves may feel the need to intentionally distinguish between personal and professional commitments when working with student activists (Griffin et al., 2019). There appears to be differential consequences for different university stakeholders, influenced by their identities, positions, and access to power.

Quaye and colleagues (2021) note that student activists may have "complicated relationships with administrators, who activists believe do not live up to their espoused values of equity and justice and, instead, often seek to placate activists or create barriers in their activism" (p. 120). Further, McCarron et al. (2024) found that a deleterious approach of educators at one's home institution can compromise the well-being of college student activists by eliciting negative affect and unpleasant emotions such as stress, anger, and frustration. In another study, participants reported a lack of support and care for them as individuals and activists, and also experienced hostility and backlash for challenging university policies and practices through their activism (Rosati et al., 2019). At its worst, students can experience the phenomenon of institutional betrayal where wrongdoings perpetrated by an institution upon individuals dependent on that institution can result in pragmatic and psychological harm (Smith & Freyd, 2014). Students report that their university served as a source of stress, a stark contrast to visible statements of higher education institutions to redouble their commitment to supporting students' mental health (Taylor, 2020). Student activists on campus may be more engaged in a wider range of issues and be more attentive to issues of self-care than prior generations of activists. Conner (2020) describes this phenomenon:

> Self-care has become a hallmark of contemporary student activism. Today's student activists certainly expose themselves to risks through their activism, including harassment, violence, and expulsion; however, they countervail this endangerment by prioritizing the taking care of themselves and one another. In their activist spaces, students have established self-care and collective care as normative practices.
>
> (p. 6)

Simultaneously, faculty and staff at universities can also be powerful sources of support for student activists. Flett and colleagues (2019) described faculty as "first-responders" who can make a profound difference in students' lives, if given the space and support to do so. Faculty may use pedagogical strategies such as community building and dialogues across differences to foster awareness of diverse perspectives and to address inequalities and to promote inclusion, and courses and activities to bolster students' sense of agency and purpose as well as enhancing their knowledge and skills. For example, Hoffman and Mitchell (2016) suggest that campus educators learn how to effectively engage in difficult discussions with student activists, including owning their power and fostering transparency. Educators should use communication tools that students are already familiar with to update and communicate with student activists (Quaye et al., 2020). McCarron and colleagues (2024) astutely note that supporting student activists does not necessarily equate with endorsing those students' agendas.

Often, universities provide students with opportunities to explore activism that were not available to them prior to college. For example, one study found that diversity courses and enrolling high numbers of students in diversity, identity, and cultural studies contributed to fostering student activism (Barnhardt, 2015). Overall, campus educators are essential contributors to the social, emotional, and overall well-being of student activists.

Findings

Findings from our research study overviewed in Chapter One of this volume are presented below, with special emphasis on how participants navigated both activist and campus communities, and the perceived effects of these environments on their well-being.

Student Activist Communities

> You know, I go out of my way to go up to every single [club member] and ask, "Hey, how are you doing this week? How are you doing? Oh, do you need help with that? Like how are you doing mentally? Are you okay? Mentally? Do you want to talk about it? Oh, you broke up with your girlfriend? Yeah, you know, let's go to Starbucks, get a coffee. Let's talk about it. I'm gonna

> give you advice. You don't want to talk about it? Okay, you know, come to my house. Let's go. You don't need to tell me … but let's get distracted a little bit" … So I had to deal not only with my own problems, not only with my own mental stress, not only with being a leader, but also with other people's mental stress problems and I don't complain about it … but I feel like it definitely adds to my mental problems. My mental situation. And it just gives me a little bit more weight. If I learned how to cope with my own stuff I feel like I will be better at coping with everyone else's. And for my [community], I want them feeling good … So for me, it's really important for people other than me to be in a good mental health space.
>
> (Violet)

Violet, a Latina student activist who shared the narrative above, described the support for and challenges to well-being inherent in her activist community. Note how student leaders may function as gatekeepers and support for the well-being of other community members.

Study participants described the additional stress that can accrue being part of activist communities. Abigail, a White woman whose activism centered on women's rights and the prevention of sexual violence, described how easy it is for burnout to occur:

> I think, when people try to take on a lot of leadership roles, they end up putting too much on their plate and I see that with a lot of the people that I ended up working with on different executive boards. So that's just like a typical student advocating for so many things at once that they just are spread thin, but also, I think specifically with the work that we're doing [which involves] a lot of really heavy content. And specifically with policy work. It can get really frustrating and like you burn out when you realize that like no matter how hard you're advocating for certain policies and how many people you're working with, and talking to about it, nothing's really changing.

However, some activist communities are increasingly cognizant of this toll. In this section's opening quote Violet described how her activist community takes proactive steps to attend to participants' well-being. She described some of these supports: "We have self-care awareness sessions. We have mental health talks and I feel like with that mental health talk it was a whole success … . Some people started telling their own problems, feeling more comfortable, feeling more like family." Elijah, a Multiracial disability rights activist, described his organization's approach:

> Once a semester we have a whole meeting dedicated to taking care of yourself, self-care, and trying to make sure that your mind, your body is good, because it's exhausting … doing activism, and just being a person with disabilities or chronic conditions in general, is a very exhausting experience.

Despite the additional pressure and stress, participants emphasized the overall significance of their activist communities, highlighting how these communities can foster support, engagement, learning, well-being, and a sense of belonging. George, a White man dedicated to promoting higher education transparency, offered insight into the sense of belonging generated in activist communities, noting:

> [In] community organizing, you make the closest bonds with people. You tell people everything. You know they're in the struggle with you together. They know everything about me. I know everything about them. It's just we always have to end up talking about our mental health. For some reason, it seems that people who care the most also are hurting the most. That's why we go into community organizing. Not only do we not want to feel this pain, we want to make sure no one else feels this pain. I think there's a lot of empathy when it comes to community organizing.

Mary A., a Latina woman whose activism focuses on racial justice, concurred stating "with activism … there's a push for real change and beneficial change and its collective. It's not just one person for their individual gain." Aaliyah, a Black woman activist for health equity, discussed the importance of community in fostering support and healing, stating: "I was exposed very young … to the power and importance of community. And, so … I wouldn't say I got involved right away just because I was a kid. I didn't really understand the weight of it."

Beyond personal and programmatic support for each other's well-being, activist communities can also serve as places of learning, growth, and development. Alexis, a Latina woman working towards criminal justice reform, emphasized the role of community in leadership, saying, "to be a leader you have to listen to your community and you have to listen to the people around you and do what's best for everybody and not just what you think is best for yourself." Leadership can also add stress though, as Abigail described above. Chloe, a Latina woman, mentioned how her work on food insecurity with the campus food pantry allows a bridging of campus and community describing it as "a tool to connect the community with the people who are in need. And we're directly observing the need and communicating that to the community so that students can get the food that they need." Edith, a White woman activist for disability rights, talked about how activist communities can evolve coalitions of support where members learn about the interconnections across oppressions. She noted:

> Even if you're not part of that community you can be an advocate working to lift those people up and kind of helping another community that you're not necessarily part of succeed, which I think extends to everything, like I simply focus on the disability community but I can still be an advocate for men of color or LGBTQ people … . I think it's really important to not focus on yourself, and focus on how you can support others.

The next section examines how study participants made meaning of institutional structures, policies, and supports.

Student Activists and Institutional Structures

> The administration has by far been the biggest hurdle to navigate at this institution. [As a result of our activism with] the defund the police movement, we were targeted by online harassment campaigns. We actually had our information and photos posted online, on hate websites. And were targeted with a massive email campaign where we were receiving emails for weeks. And the university basically just told us like, this is what you deserve for starting conversations on this issue. And you know, if you don't want to receive targeted harassment online and receive these kinds of emails, then you shouldn't be talking about this kind of stuff. And the same thing, when we first started working on these kind of

> resolutions and digging in, the admin called us in for a meeting and they were like, you know, we just really think you guys should be focusing on something that's more important to graduate students like making money and we're like, these things are all [connected], I mean, like it's disability rights, it's, you know, Black lives matter. It's all of these really key critical issues that have been such a big discussion point but so important to the community.
>
> (Chrissy)

When interviewed, Chrissy, a White woman activist, described the institutional barriers and lack of support for student activists and their well-being. Note her perception of the institution blaming student activists for the resulting harassment.

As Quaye and colleagues (2021) describe, "activists also have complicated relationships with administrators who activists believe do not live up to their espoused values of equity and justice and, instead, often seek to placate activists or create barriers in their activism" (p. 120). Certainly, institutions of higher education are often viewed as being less than responsive to student activism. Ellen, an Asian woman, described her experience trying to create more access for reproductive rights on campus:

> There may be institutional barriers. You know, when you're on a college campus, there are often cases where you want to do something really big, and there might be institutional barriers to getting certain things accomplished. And so, there might be scenarios where you'll have to kind of jump through a lot of hoops in order to get to a certain point, like sometimes you have to talk to ten different people before you find the right person … so I think sometimes institutional barriers can sometimes impede student activism.

Karen, a Latina woman passionate about environmental justice, described the challenges in learning how to navigate campus administration:

> The biggest issue is there is not a ton of institutional knowledge when it comes to activism, especially student activism on campus. It's really hard to be able to transfer that knowledge. Just learning how to deal with the bureaucracy that we have to go through. We have access to this money through being an RSO [Registered

> Student Organization], but the bureaucracy of the Student Funding Board and all of those things makes it really difficult to organize.

Abigail agreed and argued for more student representation in decision making:

> As students, we can only advocate for so much. It's really the people in power that have the decision-making [power]. So how can we make sure that our voices are heard? It is kind of just like community at large and kind of just like society … [We need to] make sure to have younger people and people that are advocating for certain things in power and in decision-making positions.

Yasmine, a Latina woman whose activism focuses on immigrant rights, advocated for enhanced flexibility in institutional structures, suggesting it is "important for the university to be a little bit more flexible with especially leaders because we're trying to guide a whole group trying to lead a whole group into doing good things not only for us but also for the university." Ely, a White man working to address food insecurity, wished university leaders would do more listening: "If you are not listening to the boots on the ground, then you're not going to get as much progress, you're not going to be as effective as you need to be." In her work for racial justice, Mary called for more respect for student opinions:

> The desires of students aren't really respected a lot of the time by administration or like changes aren't necessarily made beyond being politically correct. And you know the school still continues to like invite people to speak and do things that are inflammatory and offensive to their own student community.

Naomi concurred, stating:

> The university needs to listen to students more; they actually need to take their word seriously. They need to take action when students are promoting action and they need to stop [prioritizing] the voices of their big donors and the Board of Visitors. They need to support the people who are actually on campus. They need to support students of color, they need to support women on campus, they need to support Title IX better. There are so many issues. But

> overall, they need to listen to students. They are the ones who are on campus; they know the issues best.

Several interviewees felt that their universities did have supports in place for student activists and felt the institution cared for their well-being. Phoebe, a Black woman dedicated to civil rights, described feeling encouraged and recognized for her activism:

> I think the university recognizes the issues that students are advocating for are extremely important because I think when someone higher kinda understands what you're doing and the importance of what you're doing, that's extremely important … I think it encourages people to keep be doing what they believe and keep fighting for what they're passionate about … . I think when the university recognizes that, it gives people the motivation to keep doing what they believe in.

Violet agreed, noting: "I think that university recognition can make someone feel much better and makes them feel appreciated." Shane, an Asian man working to address health inequities, described the importance of the institution providing space for activism: "You know, a lot of what we do requires interacting with the school community, the university community. And there are certain things that the university provides, like space to do this, that is really meaningful." Veronica, a South Asian woman who focuses on mental health advocacy, suggested that "the university can definitely provide more of that tangible or like material support, or informational support, just giving information on … . counseling services at your school or like well-being tips or advice from different psychologists or professors in general." Lawrence, a White man passionate about racial justice and gender equity, "would like to see an institutionalized policy on the well-being of students."

The next section examines study participants' interactions with campus educators, including faculty, staff, and administrators.

Student Activists and Campus Educators

> How do I show up [as] non-biased towards an issue or topic and remain professional, but stay true to who I am in my beliefs, right? So, when you're working for a large university, not that you can't

> take a stance on an issue, but as a faculty, or as an administrator, you're there for all students, right? And so, I think we have to walk a fine line between supporting all students with all identities and all their beliefs, as well as what does that mean in terms of how I can show up in the workplace. So that's the first thing is a challenge is navigating higher education settings and your job, and to what extent does your job allow you to truly engage in dialogue and speak up to the things that you want to speak up to. And then I think the challenge that I have experienced within social justice work, it could get draining, right? It's a time commitment, and it's also a physical and psychological process, right? … I'll give an example—so in my department, I'm one of the only few Latinx professionals in my area. And, as we're thinking about how do we move towards being more inclusive and more aware and more equitable in our processes, if you don't have that many people of color on your staff, you're probably going to keep going to the same people to help talk about diversity, equity, work and so sometimes it can be taxing that a small group of people are always the people that people are going to address an issue when it comes to a topic around diversity, equity and inclusion.
>
> (Phil)

In his interview, Phil, a Latino graduate student advocated for marginalized student populations, offered the narrative above describing the challenges campus educators may face in supporting student activist well-being.

Behind institutional policies and procedures are individual educators and administrators whose approach and commitments can affect student activists' well-being. Engaging in coursework relevant to a student activists' interests, especially when accompanied by supportive faculty, provides support to student activist well-being. George described the positive impact of taking courses related to mindfulness and well-being in college, stating:

> I consider myself very fortunate to have spent a lot of time engaging in education spaces around mindfulness and well-being. I took many courses here as an undergrad student around those themes specifically and did a lot of additional coursework with faculty here in their certificate programs around that deep reflection and mindfulness. I think that the lessons that I learned through that

> and the relationship that I've built with [the faculty] … a lot of it is about building a really strong relationship with yourself and being able to recognize the signs of when something needs to shift and change and learning to listen to that intuition in that space. I feel really grateful that I was able to learn those lessons and engage in that work before diving into this, because I don't know that I would have been able to recognize that a change needed to be made and been able to feel empowered enough and competent enough to make those shifts had I not had that background. I think it's something that everyone should [experience].

Naomi described how learning about intersectionality in an academic course advanced her activism. She recalled, "I took a Women's Studies class, about gender and society. That's where we kind of talked about intersectionality being implemented in the creation of Black feminism and lesbian feminism and stuff, and it was just really powerful." Daphne, a public health science major and Cameroonian-American woman, noted how doing research with a faculty member sparked her activism:

> I don't even know how I got into this but I spoke to a professor and I started doing the research with her and it got me interested in the relationship between public health and information science so I'm now a Public Health and Information Science major and I think that's what really got me interested in this realm because it's a combination of like health advocacy science and environmental science and different things.

Benjamin, who identifies as non-binary, attended a Title One middle school and a Title One high school and mentioned how his activism was influenced by courses and educational experiences, noting: "I wanted to know why I lived in an area that was fairly affluent, but the high school I went to and the middle school I went to were underrepresented or didn't have the adequate resources." Chloe reflected on the impact of a specific course: "I took a course on social justice that really opened my eyes to a lot of the issues that I now focus on in my activism. The professor was very engaging and encouraged us to think critically about the material." In contrast to his prior comment on the power of classroom support, George admitted there are challenges to engaging in academic spaces as an activist:

> Trying to maintain a space with compassion for people who are in different places in their social justice journey and trying to operate from that space to do social justice work can be challenging at times, especially in a classroom setting where you have students who are saying really problematic things in a class in an open setting. Trying to find a balance between combating that problematic information and trying to steer towards a space of justice without marginalizing that student or making them feel like they don't belong in that space or there's no value in what they're saying. Also recognizing how the language that they're speaking is sending that message to other students in the classroom who may be occupying an identity that is marginalized by that speech. It's a very delicate tightrope to walk.

Susan, a White woman whose activism focuses on transparency in higher education, and Elijah expressed gratitude for faculty who understand the demands activism can place on students. Susan stated, "faculty are usually very understanding when it comes to us needing extensions for assignments due to our activism work, but it's not always guaranteed." Elijah concurred, noting, "I have had the support of some faculty members who understand the importance of our work and provide the necessary flexibility. However, it is not a universal experience, and it can be challenging to balance responsibilities." Axel, a racial justice activist who identifies as non-binary, shared how he integrated activism into coursework, commenting, "I've had a lot of professors who have been very supportive of my activism. They've allowed me to integrate my activism into my coursework, which has been incredibly helpful."

Chloe, a social work student, underscores the power of faculty and administrators as mentors as she works to address food insecurity:

> A lot of my professors have been personally been involved in activism. So a lot of the times they give us tips on how to manage it, or how to like, separate our personal life from our work to, you know, take care of your own self. You know, we talk a lot about self-care, and it's obviously different to learn about it and actually be able to put it into practice. But just like knowing that you have those tools and learning how other people have managed it, I think has been really helpful … I think a lot of my professors have been,

> like mentors to me, or have been a really good resource to learn how to manage that. And my supervisors as well. A lot of them have been involved in food insecurity for a long time. They've been like personally involved with the pantry and like starting the pantry so like I said they're professionals within the area. And learning from them has been really helpful.

Discussion and Implications for Research and Practice

This section connects the insights from participants to the extant literature on activist communities, institutional structures, and campus educators. Overall themes include: Activist communities functioning as an important bridge between self-care and collective care; a call for listening, authenticity, and transparency in campus decision making; and an emphasis on how individual educators and administrators can be instrumental to student activists' well-being. Institutions of higher education could frame their relationship to student activists as community partners, which could allow for enhanced reciprocity and student well-being.

Communities

In their personal narratives, participants emphasized the role of on- and off-campus activist communities in enhancing their well-being, as conceptualized by Diener (2009) in terms of "pleasant emotions" such as joy, contentment, and happiness. They highlight the positive experiences derived from socializing, engaging in artistic endeavors, watching movies, and simply being part of a community outside their activist work. Further, it seems that activist communities are waking up to the fact that intentional programming and support for well-being are vital. Several participants describe their organizations hosting self-care awareness sessions, mental health talks, and authentic discussions about how to avoid or address activist burnout. This is not to imply that the "culture of martyrdom" (Gorski & Chen, 2015, Rodgers, 2010) no longer exists in these organizations, or even may exist contemporaneously with programs and support for well-being. Either way, the very presence of community seems to foster feelings of solidarity and support; as George described earlier, community organizing can foster close bonds prompted by the feeling of being "in the struggle with you together."

Study participants describe various entrance paths to finding a supportive activist community. Some, like Aaliyah, were raised in activist families and communities, and grew more aware about how to access those communities' resources and support as they got older. Others, like Edith, were introduced to communities by friends and peers. Many interviewees described their evolution of involvement and belonging as moving from being a mere participant or sporadic attendee at community programs and events, to gradually taking on responsibilities within the organization, and finally stepping into leadership roles within the community. Future scholarship should explore the additional burdens and stressors accrued by serving in leadership positions within activist communities. Several participants, including Abigail and Violet, mentioned that feeling responsible for the well-being of others placed additional stressors on their own well-being.

Beyond personal and programmatic support for members, activist communities also served as places of learning, growth, and development. In their interviews, students described learning more about issues they care about from participating in activist communities, forming coalitions of support across activist communities, and deepening relationships that are essential for social, emotional, and practical reciprocity. Activist communities that promote self-care are also engaging in collective care and building both individual and organizational endurance for sustained engagement.

Institutional Structures

It was not surprising that participants expressed frustration with institutional responses to their activism, and that the barriers and bureaucracy of institutional structures detracted from student activist well-being. The list of institutional roadblocks described was long and included: Colleges being non-responsive to student requests for change and maintaining the status quo (Naomi); responding to change efforts in superficial or mitigative ways rather than making real transformation (Chrissy); and employing delay tactics designed to push decision making to break periods or even to draw out decision making until activists have graduated or new issues have supplanted old requests for change (George). It was interesting that participants echoed the scholarship in seeking congruence between the rhetoric espoused by institutions of higher education, and what is actually enacted on campuses (Quaye et al., 2020). Participants wanted universities to live out the values they publicly proclaim. Recall Lawrence's dream that his campus would develop a formalized policy on the well-being of students.

Other ideas from students about how institutions could better support the well-being of activists include: Facilitating student activist organizations in transferring knowledge across leadership and academic transitions (Karen); including more student representation in decision making (Abigail); enhanced flexibility in institutional structures (Yasmine); more access to psychological services and well-being programs (Veronica); providing safe space for gatherings of student activists (Shane); and an overwhelming call for university leaders to spend more time listening to and communicating transparently with students. Ely, Mary, Naomi, and others called for institutions to value student voices as much as administrators value donors, Board of Visitors members, and the like. It seems a simple request from student activists—to be listened to, taken seriously, and acknowledged for their efforts to try and make institutions of higher education to be more just, equitable, and inclusive spaces. It was heartening that several interviewees noted that their universities did have support in place for student activists, made them feel appreciated, and felt the institution cared for their well-being.

Campus Educators

When queried about institutional responses that support or hindered activists' well-being, participants invariably shared stories of barriers and burdens, but when asked about the effects of individual campus educators on their well-being, most students shared powerful and positive stories about individual faculty, staff, and administrators. This supports the emerging scholarship that highlights campus educators are pivotal to student activists' sense of social and emotional support, and to their overall sense of well-being (McCarron et al., 2024). Participants frequently named educators who shared and understood their experiences and identities as being especially pivotal, underscoring findings from Chávez and Ramrakhiani (2021) and Quaye and colleagues (2017).

Student activists engaging in course work and research that related to their ideologies and interests was especially important in advancing their own activism and sense of self. Narratives from Naomi, Daphne,

Benjamin, Chloe, and others, detailed how engaging in relevant coursework with caring and committed faculty could advance their own development and engagement. Interestingly, several participants (Susan, Elijah, Axel) expressed gratitude for faculty who understood the demands activism can place on students, and who allowed for flexibility and individualization in course work. This seems in line with research indicating Gen Z students' preferences for academic flexibility (Seemiller & Grace, 2016). Chloe's view of her professors and on-campus supervisors as resources and mentors suggests a roadmap for future faculty development.

Conclusion

Activist communities can both nurture or deplete their members' well-being. Study participants described the profound sense of camaraderie and belonging nurtured in these communities. They also decried the occasional culture of martyrdom and the frequent lack of intentional structures and supports for activist well-being. Study participants had similar feelings about campus communities. When taken together, the diversity of policies, programs, and pedagogies on campus, coupled with the wide variety of motivations of institutional actors, can make it challenging to map productive strategies to enhance student activist well-being. One approach to examining the complex interplay between campus, community, and student activism is to apply the SOFAR model that elucidates relations between students (S), organization representatives (O), faculty (F), administrators (A), and residents (R) (Bringle et al., 2009). Developed to enhance campus–community partnerships focused on civic engagement, the model allows for a nuanced mapping of the partnerships necessary to make change. The quality of these partnerships is assessed by the degree to which the interactions possess closeness, equity, and integrity, and the degree to which the outcomes of those interactions are exploitive, transactional, or transformational.

By illuminating the multiplicity of roles these communities play in enhancing well-being and exacerbating stress, campus educators can begin to make necessary interventions. Adopting a partnership approach underscores the importance of fostering supportive environments within colleges and universities, where student activists can find solace, encouragement, and a sense of belonging. Additionally, this approach may emphasize the need for institutions to address the challenges faced by student activists, acknowledging their contributions and providing the necessary support for their holistic well-being. The resources and thought questions below provide a starting point. Activist scholar bell hooks suggests that educators can be sources of hope and creators of supportive communities (hooks, 2003). Parker Palmer (1998) shares his vision for college campuses to be sites of healing and well-being:

> Community goes far beyond our face-to-face relationship with each other as human beings. In education especially, community connects us with what Rilke called "the grace of great things" … . we are in community with all these great things. Great teaching is about knowing and feeling that community, and then drawing your students into it.
>
> (p. 3)

Scholarship in Action
Community: Bridging Self and Collective Care

Thought Questions:

For students: How do your activist communities (both on- and off-campus) empower or constrain your personal well-being? What specific actions are your communities taking to support personal and organizational well-being?

For staff/practitioners: How do you balance your personal identities and commitments with your professional identities and commitments when working with student activists? Is it possible to both reflect/uphold the institution's policies and decisions while simultaneously supporting students working to change or challenge those policies and decisions? How is your own well-being affected by navigating these multiple responsibilities and commitments?

For faculty: In what ways does your own research, scholarship, service, and teaching reflect your own commitments and values? How are you inviting students to explore their own ideologies and commitments through your teaching and scholarship? Are there appropriate intersections of faculty and student activism in holding institutions accountable? How do your course policies and expectations empower or constrain the well-being of student activists?

For community partners: How do your organizational policies and practices empower or constrain the well-being of involved student activists? What specific actions could your organization take to support individual and collective well-being? Is the link between personal well-being and organizational sustainability evident to participants and partners?

For researchers: Are there ways to engage in scholar-activism through your own research activities? To what degree are you conducting identity- and power-responsive research? How might you engage students, staff, and community partners in the work of research for social change? Do you disseminate your scholarly research results in ways that are translatable across contexts and communities?

Resources for Additional Learning:

Assessment Tools:

Consider results from large- and small-scale measures of community well-being. Some measure socio-economic well-being, while others measure physical and mental health outcomes. A campus measure of equity and inclusion is also listed below.

Human Well-Being Index (U.S.)
https://catalog.data.gov/dataset/human-well-being-index-hwbi-for-u-s-counties
Gallup National Health and Well-Being Index (U.S.)
https://wellbeingindex.sharecare.com/
National Assessment of Collegiate Campus Climates (NACC)
https://race.usc.edu/colleges/naccc/

Websites:

Campus Compact—Includes searchable programs and resources for students, faculty, staff, and community partners related to activism and community engagement
www.compact.org

Conferences:

IMPACT conference
www.impactconference.org/

Books:

Conner, J. O. (2020). *The new student activists: The rise of neoactivism on college campuses*. Johns Hopkins University Press.

Conner explores the recent uptick in student activism on college campuses. Rather than deriding activists as either "snowflakes" or "justice warriors," Conner moves beyond these simple stereotypes and convenient caricatures to examine the nuanced motives and complex experiences of real-life, present-day college student activists. Social and educational influences on sociopolitical development are explored.

Morgan, D. L., & Davis, C. (Eds.). (2019). *Student activism, politics, and campus climate in higher education.* Routledge.

This volume presents a comprehensive, contemporary portrait of political engagement and student activism at postsecondary institutions in the United States. Its many insightful contributors explore how colleges and universities are experiencing unrest and in what ways broader socio-political conflicts are evident on-campus, ultimately unpacking the political dimensions of student engagement within campus climates.

Articles:

Bringle, R. G., Clayton, P. H., & Price, M. (2009). Partnerships in service learning and civic engagement. *Partnerships: A Journal of Service Learning & Civic Engagement*, *1*(1), 1–20. [SOFAR model]

Quaye, S. J., Lange, A. C., Benbow, R. J., Pfund, C., Thayer-Hart, N., & Branchaw, J. (2020). Pete's letter: A student activist's message to campus administrators. *Journal of Diversity in Higher Education, 13*(3), 240–253. https://doi.org/10.1037/dhe0000293

Classroom Activities:

Consider applying this toolkit for community-engaged wellness mapping to your classroom or activist organization.

https://in.nau.edu/wp-content/uploads/sites/8/2018/09/Wellness-Mapping-2014-CES4Health.pdf

References

Baker, D. J., & Blissett, R. S. L. (2018). Beyond the incident: Institutional predictors of student collective action. *Journal of Higher Education, 89*(2), 184–207. https://doi.org/10.1080/00221546.2017.1368815

Barnett, K., Ropers-Huilman, R., & Aaron, L. (2008). A planning-process perspective on student activists' upward influence attempts to effect campus change. *Southern Communication Journal, 73*(4), 332–346. https://doi.org/10.1080/10417940802418833

Barnhardt, C. L. (2015). Campus educational contexts and civic participation: Organizational links to collective action. *Journal of Higher Education, 86*(1), 38–70. https://doi.org/10.1080/00221546.2015.11777356

Barnhardt, C. L., Sheets, J. E., & Pasquesi, K. (2015). You expect what? Students' perceptions as resources in acquiring commitments and capacities for civic engagement. *Research in Higher Education, 56*, 622–644. https://doi.org/10.1007/s11162-014-9361-8

Binder, A. J., & Kidder, J. L. (2022). *The channels of student activism: How the left and right are winning (and losing) in campus politics today.* University of Chicago Press.

Bringle, R. G., Clayton, P. H., & Price, M. (2009). Partnerships in service learning and civic engagement. *Partnerships: A Journal of Service Learning & Civic Engagement, 1*(1), 1–20. https://doi.org/10.7253/partj.v1i1.415

Broadhurst, C., & Martin, G. L. (2014). Part of the "establishment"? Fostering positive campus climates for student activists. *Journal of College and Character, 15*(2), 75–86. https://doi.org/10.1515/jcc-2014-0012

Byrd, W. C., Luney, L. T., Marie, J., & Sanders, K. N. (2019). Demanding attention: An exploration of institutional characteristics of recent student demands. *Journal of Diversity in Higher Education*, *14*(1), 25–36. https://doi.org/10.1037/dhe0000133

Chávez, M., & Ramrakhiani, S. (2021). Resist: An exploration of student activists' partnerships with faculty and student affairs. *Journal of Student Affairs Research and Practice*, *58*(5), 520–531. https://doi.org/10.1080/19496591.2020.1784748

Chen, C., & Gorski, P. (2015). Burnout in social justice and human rights activists: Symptoms, causes and implications. *Journal of Human Rights Practice*, *7*(3), 366–390. https://doi.org/10.1093/jhuman/huv011

Chen, C., McCarron, G. P., & Owen, J. E. (2024). The emotional labor of college student activism: An interview-based study. *Journal of Human Rights Practice*. https://doi.org/10.1093/jhuman/huae025

Conner, J. O. (2020). *The new student activists: The rise of neoactivism on college campuses*. Johns Hopkins University Press. https://doi.org/10.5195/rt.2020.838

Diener, E. (2009). Subjective well-being. In E. Diener (Ed.), *The science of well-being: The collected works of Ed Diener* (pp. 11–58). Springer. https://doi.org/10.1007/978-90-481-2350-6_2

Flett, J., Hayne, H., Riordan, B. C., Thompson, L. M., & Conner, T. S. (2019). Mobile mindfulness meditation: A randomized controlled trial of the effect of two popular apps on mental health. *Mindfulness*, *10*(5), 863–876. https://doi.org/10.1007/s12671-018-1050-9

Gomes, M. (1992). The rewards and stresses of social change: A qualitative study of peace activists. *Journal of Humanistic Psychology*, *32*(4), 138–146.

Gorski, P. C., & Chen, C. (2015). "Frayed all over": The causes and consequences of activist burnout among social justice education activists. *Educational Studies: Journal of the American Educational Studies Association*, *51*(5), 385–405. https://doi.org/10.1080/00131946.2015.1075989

Griffin, K. A., Hart, J. L., Worthington, R. L., Belay, K., & Yeung, J. G. (2019). Race-related activism: How do higher education diversity professionals respond? *The Review of Higher Education*, *43*(2), 667–696. https://doi.org/10.1353/rhe.2019.0114

Grim, J. K., Lee, N. L., Museus, S. D., Na, V. S., & Ting, M. P. (2019). Asian American college student activism and social justice in Midwest contexts. *New Directions for Higher Education*, *186*, 25–36. https://doi.org/10.1002/he.20321

Hoffman, G. D., & Mitchell, T. D. (2016). Making diversity "everyone's business": A discourse analysis of institutional responses to student activism for equity and inclusion. *Journal of Diversity in Higher Education*, *9*(3), 277–289. https://doi.org/10.1037/dhe0000037

hooks, b. (2003). *Teaching community: A pedagogy of hope*. Routledge.

Hopgood, S. (2006). *Keepers of the flame: Understanding Amnesty International*. Cornell University Press.

Kezar, A., Gallant, T. B., & Lester, J. (2011). Everyday people making a difference on college campuses: The tempered grassroots leadership tactics of faculty and staff. *Studies in Higher Education, 36*(2), 129–151. https://doi.org/10.1080/03075070903532304

Kovan, J. T., & Dirkx, J. M. (2003). "Being called awake": The role of transformative learning in the lives of environmental activists. *Adult Education Quarterly, 53*(2), 99–118. https://doi.org/10.1177/0741713602238906

Linder, C. (2019). Power-conscious and intersectional approaches to supporting student activists: Considerations for learning and development. *Journal of Diversity in Higher Education, 12*(1), 17–26. https://doi.org/10.1037/dhe0000082

Linder, C., Quaye, S. J., Lange, A. C., Roberts, R. E., Lacy, M. C., & Okello, W. K. (2019a). "A student should have the privilege of just being a student": Student activism as labor. *The Review of Higher Education, 42*(5), 37–62. https://doi.org/10.1353/rhe.2019.0044

Linder, C., Quaye, S. J., Stewart, T. J., Okello, W. K., & Roberts, R. E. (2019b). "The whole weight of the world on my shoulders": Power, identity, and student activism. *Journal of College Student Development, 60*(5), 527–542. https://doi.org/10.1353/csd.2019.0048

Lorde, A. (1988). *A burst of light*. Firebrand Books.

Maslach, C., & Gomes, M. E. (2006). Overcoming burnout. In R. M. MacNair (Ed.), *Working for peace: A handbook of practical psychology and other tools* (2nd Ed., pp. 43–49). Impact Publishers.

Maslach, C., & Leiter, M. P. (2005). Reversing burnout: How to rekindle your passion for your work. *Stanford Social Innovation Review, 3*(4), 42–49.

McCarron, G. P., Chen, C. W., April, J., & LaMagdeleine, I. (2024). An exploratory study of the relationship between college student activists' labor and their subjective well-being: Perspectives from a U.S. institution. *Journal of American College Health*, 1–10. Online First. https://doi.org/10.1080/07448481.2024.2338409

McCarron, G. P., Chen, C. W., Blanton, S., Guerrieri, G., Lucioni, R. G., Gurung, E., Sreevals, A., & Enciu, J. (2023). College student activists' perceptions of mattering to campus educators. *Journal of Student Affairs Research and Practice, 61*(3), 368–384. https://doi.org/10.1080/19496591.2023.2201195

Miller, M. T., & Tolliver III, D. V. (2017). *Student activism as a vehicle for change on college campuses: Emerging research and opportunities*. IGI Global. https://doi.org/10.4018/978-1-5225-2173-0

Ozbay, F., Johnson D. C., Dimoulas, E., Morgan, C. A., Charney, D., & Southwick, S. (2007). Social support and resilience to stress: From neurobiology to clinical practice. *Psychiatry, 4*(5), 35–40. PMID: 20806028.

Palmer, P. (September, 1998). The grace of great things: Reclaiming the sacred in knowing, teaching, and learning. *The Sun*. www.thesunmagazine.org/issues/273/the-grace-of-great-things

Quaye, S. J., Lange, A. C., Benbow, R. J., Pfund, C., Thayer-Hart, N., & Branchaw, J. (2020). Pete's letter: A student activist's message to campus administrators. *Journal of Diversity in Higher Education*, *13*(3), 240–253. https://doi.org/10.1037/dhe0000293

Quaye, S. J., Linder, C., Stewart, T. J., & Satterwhite, E. M. (2021). A critical examination of college student activism from 2000-2020. In L. W. Perna (Ed.), *Higher education: Handbook of theory and research* (pp. 81–132). Springer.

Quaye, S. J., Shaw, M. D., & Hill, D. C. (2017). Blending scholar and activist identities: Establishing the need for scholar activism. *Journal of Diversity in Higher Education*, *10*(4), 381–399. https://doi.org/10.1037/dhe0000060

Renn, K. A. (2007). LGBT Student leaders and queer activists: Identities of lesbian, gay, bisexual, transgender, and queer identified college student leaders and activists. *Journal of College Student Development*, *48*(3), 311–330. https://doi.org/10.1353/csd.2007.0029

Rhoads, R. (1998a). *Freedom's web: Activism in an age of cultural diversity*. Johns Hopkins University Press.

Rhoads, R. (1998b). Student protest and multicultural reform: Making sense of campus unrest in the 1990s. *The Journal of Higher Education*, *69*(6), 621–646. https://doi.org/10.2307/2649211

Rodgers, K. (2010). "Anger is why we're all here": Mobilizing and managing emotions in a professional activist organization. *Social Movement Studies*, *9*, 273–291. https://doi.org/10.1080/14742837.2010.493660

Ropers-Huilman, B., Carwile, L., & Barnett, K. (2005). Student activists' characterizations of administrators in higher education: Perceptions of power in "the system." *The Review of Higher Education*, *28*(3), 295–312. https://doi.org/10.1353/rhe.2005.0012

Rosati, C., Nguyen, D. J., Troyer, R., Tran, Q., Graman, Z., & Brenckle, J. (2019). Exploring how student activists experience marginality and mattering during interactions with student affairs professionals. *College Student Affairs Journal*, *37*(2), 113–127. https://doi.org/10.1353/csj.2019.0009

Schaufeli, W. B., & Buunk, P. (2002). Burnout: An overview of 25 years of research and theorizing. In M. J. Schabracq, J. A. M. Winnubst, & C. L. Cooper (Eds.), *The handbook of work and health psychology* (pp. 383–425). Wiley.

Seemiller, C., & Grace, M. (2016). *Generation Z goes to college*. Jossey-Bass.

Smith, C. P., & Freyd, J. J. (2014). Institutional betrayal. *American Psychologist*, *69*(6), 575–587. https://doi.org/10.1037/a0037564

Taylor, S. (2020, April 28). In the age of coronavirus, student activism is more relevant than ever. The Education Trust. https://edtrust.org/resource/in-the-age-of-coronavirus-student-activism-is-more-relevant-than-ever/

Tolliver, D. V., Miller, M. T., Miles, J. M., & Nadler, D. P. (2018). Faculty and student activism: Parallel courses or divergent paths. In M. T. Miller & D. V. Tolliver (Eds.), *Exploring the technological, societal, and institutional dimensions of college student activism* (pp. 183–195). IGI Global. https://doi.org/10.4018/978-1-5225-7274-9.ch011

6 Reflection, Synthesis, and the Way Forward

> *I just think that as a culture we don't really acknowledge self-care as important as it should be. Even now I'm much more hesitant to say that I need to check in myself as I am to say that my friends need to check in with themselves. I'm like, oh, you guys really need to take care of yourselves and then I just don't [do it for myself]. I don't know how to explain it, I just think that it's the way that we've all grown up that physically sick days are more important than mentally sick days. I think that culture is shifting but our generation was kind of the last one to not really accept it so I don't know. And that's something that I'm struggling with myself too is that I always say that I'll take a month off from that [activism] and I just don't, because I don't have the privilege or the time to do that. And then I think there's also a bunch of socio-economic reasons as to why mental health isn't really taken care of. I don't think that's so much of an activist reason, but I think that's a whole other conversation.*—Lily

Lily, a 20-year-old White woman whose student activism centered on menstrual equity and the prevention of gender-based violence, described both personal and systemic roadblocks to valuing self-care and well-being. Lily posited it as a generational issue, but also conveyed how issues of identity, power, and privilege may shape activists' access to resources that bolster well-being. This concluding chapter synthesizes findings from our study of the experiences of 119 U.S. college student activists and examines how they attributed meaning to their activism and well-being. In their interviews, participants shared the personal costs and risks associated with their activism, as well as the factors that either mitigated or exacerbated their well-being. Notably, the significant costs related to time emerged as a prominent theme,

DOI: 10.4324/9781003481010-6

alongside the dangers and risks of burnout. Using Bronfenbrenner's (1977, 1996) ecological model as a frame, we examine the embedded and intricate relationships among self-care, activist communities, and the larger university environment, discovering that the meaning student activists ascribed to their activism was multifaceted, intertwined with both triumph and loss, and influenced by their multiple and intersecting identities.

Introduction

This text explores the experience and well-being of students who meet the broad definition of student activists. In Chapter One, we introduced the study that serves as the foundation for this text including key literature, theoretical underpinnings, the methodology, and our philosophy. The nuanced and complex discussion related to how students benefit from participating in student activism is our focus in Chapter Two. In Chapter Three, we uncovered how college student activists interpret the relationship between their social identity and working for social change. A notable concern for student activists is the risk of burnout, which we pursue in Chapter Four. Lastly, Chapter Five examines the multifaceted and complex ways that communities both support and can inhibit the work of student activists. The present chapter serves as a reflection and synthesis of what we shared in this volume and focuses on the implications of our research and policy recommendations from several disciplinary frames.

There are many noteworthy and memorable contributions from our study participants. As detailed in earlier chapters, they balanced their growing understanding of their social identities with activism that emerged from those identities. They contributed to local communities and were advocates for regional, national, and even international concerns. They engaged in campus-based community-building and served as confidants and supporters for their peers. In their multiple roles, they served as "bridge builders" between campuses and communities. Our participants were also repairers and initiators, helping campuses and communities align values, policies, and actions. Their efforts took place on multiple and intersecting levels. As researchers, it was incumbent upon us to acknowledge how our participants' positionalities influenced their roles and activism, and how the climate of the multiple communities to which they belonged affected their experience and well-being.

For this final chapter, we propose an additional frame to serve as a vehicle for making meaning of the various ways in which students pursued activism and perceived the effects of that activism. Using an ecological model that highlights the ways that students interacted with their environments, we seek to illuminate themes present in our participants' organizing, convening, and advocacy. Examining our participants through an ecological lens allows us to attend to the multiple and intersecting levels of their interactions.

An Ecological Frame

Bronfenbrenner's ecological systems theory (1977, 1996) suggested that we can understand how students develop by attending to their interactions with friends, family members, teachers, administrators, and communities as well as policies and institutions. Bronfenbrenner (1993) proposed "a system of nested, interdependent, dynamic structures ranging from the proximal, consisting of immediate face-to-face settings, to the most distal, comprising broader social contexts such as classes and culture" (p. 4). This constant person–environment interaction results in development. To better understand the results of these interactions, Bronfenbrenner identified the various levels as microsystems, mesosystems, exosystems, macrosystems, and chronosystems. An individual interacts with multiple microsystems reflecting their most proximal context, which could include the people with whom they live such as family members or roommates, members of their student organizations, co-workers, and fellow students in their major (Renn & Arnold, 2003). These immediate contexts can facilitate and constrain student behaviors as well as promoting and inhibiting student self-awareness and instincts to participate in student activism. In the microsystem individuals are likely to consider how their behaviors align with the espoused values and actions of others in their immediate community.

The mesosystem contains various microsystems (Bronfenbrenner, 1977, 1996). Students' interactions with these different microsystems may involve inconsistencies, leading students "to confront contradictory processes and messages between individual microsystems" (Renn & Arnold, 2003, p. 271). The exosystem represents the impact of organizational cultures such as university policies and actions as well as larger systems such as municipal, state, and federal government laws, policies, and actors. It also includes broader systems such as media, economic policy, and religious bodies. Societal norms, as well as cultural beliefs and values, are reflected in the macrosystem. The chronosystem reflects the effects of time, socio-historical conditions, and life events. Given the salience of microsystems to the lived experiences of the college student activists who shared their voice in this text, in the following we tease apart the microsystem and mesosystem and its relationship with college student activist well-being, writ large. We further elaborate on the place of exosystems, macrosystems, and chronosystems with respect to activist embeddedness and paths to liberation.

Navigating Microsystems: The Influence of Relationships on Subjective Well-Being

Our participants described specific relationships that affected their subjective well-being (SWB; Diener, 2009), and, in this section, we examine those experiences through the lens of the microsystem. We also contextualize participants' reports with the scholarship of student activism to highlight how our most immediate relationships play a crucial role in student activists' well-being.

Sense of Belonging

Experiencing a sense of belonging is critical not only to persistence in higher education (Ellison & Braxton, 2023), but it can also be a precursor to SWB. Participants reported feelings of fulfillment from collaborating with individuals with whom they shared the goal of social change. Pierce's (2021) research supported this finding of meaningful increases in the sense of belonging. When minoritized students organize to create a student community where limited or no connections are present, they are growing a sense of belonging for themselves and others (Linder et al., 2020; Nicolazzo, 2016; Warnock & Hurst, 2016). The peer connections inherent in activism serve as a protective factor against the concerning mental and physical health struggles inherent in social isolation that is pervasive on college campuses (Evans & Fisher, 2022).

Chapter Two presented examples from our participants and the literature of students who persisted despite inhospitable college environments. These students faced hostility and ambivalence due to their social identities, but responded with efforts to improve the community. In Nicolazzo's (2016) study of trans students at a large research university, she described collaborating with her participants to redefine the notion of resilience from a noun to a verb. Even if trans students did not feel resilient, they could still practice resilience notwithstanding the antagonistic milieu. While the feelings associated with this experience would likely be unpleasant (Diener, 2009), the activism would lead to meaning-making and possibly to fulfillment. The microsystems of peer relationships, in addition to the connections highlighted by Nicolazzo, were essential to well-being.

Positive relationships with faculty members are another example of microsystems that reinforce well-being. In a related study, McCarron and colleagues (2023) found that faculty contributed to student activists' feeling that they were being paid attention to, that others cared about their successes and failures, and that they could be relied upon. These are the ingredients of mattering. Faculty attended to students by connecting them to resources, demonstrated care by looking out for their well-being, assisted them by sharing unique elements of the college or university culture, and showed respect for student insights and intelligence by inviting them as student researchers and valued contributors (McCarron et al., 2023). Even when our participants were troubled by instances where they felt it was their responsibility to "repair" mistakes and problems initiated by university staff, adjusting their class schedule to accommodate their commitments to activism, and tolerating actions that did not live up to promises and pronouncements, the ways that faculty boosted student mattering served as a counternarrative to frustrations and disappointments.

Social and Activist Identities

As detailed in Chapter Three, most participants could not separate their activism from their identities and their immediate relationships or microsystems. That is, many of the participants expressed how their struggle in solidarity with other students was critical to helping them articulate their identities. Understandably, many of our participants found these experiences of marginalization unpleasant. While some of these feelings laid the groundwork for more positive emotions, these feelings did not alleviate the unfairness and frustrations associated with the additional toll marginalized student activists face.

Soloman (2014) illuminated how troubling, unjust, and unfair experiences of abuse and oppression are never deserved and can never be rationalized, but they can become part of a new narrative. He argued that: "Identity involves entering a community to draw strength from that community, and to give strength there" (Soloman, 2014, para. 7). This process of simultaneously authoring a more complex narrative while dialoguing with a community about that identity is reflective of Bronfenbrenner's (1977, 1996) notion of the mesosystem. Participants spoke of balancing their understanding of their identity as they interacted with peers who shared similarities and differences. Soloman (2014) suggested that: "We don't seek the painful experiences that hew our identities, but we seek our identities in the wake of painful experiences" (para. 16).

Participants found meaning in the mesosystem by forging ahead through the inconsistencies of their complex microsystems and articulating their previously silenced identities. This more public claiming of identity involved simultaneously putting oneself at risk for social marginalization and the positive emotions of exercising agency. As students seek the language to articulate an activist identity they may also initially demarcate specific boundaries around what it does and does not mean to be themselves. This tight circumscription around a set of acts in which to perform or a very particular cause could set students up for confusion and emptiness if their behaviors become misaligned with their definition. For example, if activist demands are accommodated by the institution, the student may struggle with issues of both identity and purpose. If a student's sole identity was based on being seen as an activist, they may still exhibit specific performative aspects to satisfy or demonstrate to members of their microsystem that they are truly an activist.

Members of students' microsystems, such as faculty members and administrators, can support students in responding to the complexity of identity construction. They can acknowledge the primacy of social identities, the complexity and uniqueness of those identities, and the role of inequity and power differentials. Additionally, trusted individuals can facilitate student activists' understanding of the importance of building an activist identity on a foundation of values (Gervais, 2023), not only on performing specific behaviors.

The Risk of Burnout

Our exploration of the burdens of activism and the risk of burnout in Chapter Four of this volume unearthed the importance of community and emotional support for student activists. Participants discussed, and the larger literature addresses, the sense of responsibility and high expectations that student activists impose on themselves to make change. The stakes are often high for the communities in which the activists are advocating, which brings additional stress. Participants acknowledged that they are susceptible to the feeling that, without their leadership or contribution, the issue for which they worked so hard, the cause or movement may fail. The feeling that the success of the effort rests on the shoulders of any particular student can be a much-needed jolt to a student's self-esteem, but it can also devolve into a sense of martyrdom (Gorski & Chen, 2015; Rodgers, 2010) or unproductive narcissism.

As noted, minoritized students are also burdened with disentangling the various and intertwining strands of oppression. When other members of the students' microsystems do not understand the seriousness of their concerns and the feeling of hopelessness that may undergird these struggles, students can be left feeling deflated and misunderstood. Minoritized students are even more susceptible to these challenging feelings when privileged members of their microsystems do not possess an awareness of the impacts of oppression. Feeling misunderstood and not supported can lead to student isolation from other members of their microsystems, which is a warning sign for poor mental and physical health.

Self-care practices that connect students to members of their microsystem outside of day-to-day activist efforts have been shown to interrupt feelings of burnout. At first blush, this finding seems paradoxical compared with the earlier assertion that student activists are emboldened by the sense of belonging they find with fellow student activists. However, these outcomes, in fact, support each other. Student activists need to have varied and diverse microsystems and ensure that their mesosystem is a sphere where they are not siloed into specific microsystems. That is, student activists' well-being is bolstered when faculty and staff recognize their many identities and multiple community memberships.

Too often administrators and faculty are guilty of blaming student activists for the disruptions they instigate instead of recognizing and highlighting embedded systems of unfairness and injustice. Supporting the well-being of students can partially be accomplished through encouraging student self-care, but as participants acknowledged, administrators often make these calls as performative speech. Perhaps more meaningful is when faculty and administrators work to raise awareness of societal unfairness and how basic human rights should not be doled out as privileges, but available to all (Gay, 2022).

The Interplay of Micro- and Mesosystems: Organizational and Institutional Factors in Student Activist Well-Being

The intra- and interpersonal developmental effects of activism on well-being are shaped by individuals' embeddedness in organizational and institutional systems and structures. Bronfenbrenner (1992) refers to these forces as the microsystem and the interactions between different microsystems as the mesosystem. No matter how intentional an individual activist may be in guarding their well-being, there are organizational and institutional forces that can either support or hinder their efforts. Chapter Five of this volume examined the role of communities—specifically activist and university communities—in shaping student activists' identities, sense of belonging, understanding of social issues, and overall well-being.

Many of the participants in our study lamented the deleterious effects of communities on their well-being. In their descriptions of their activist organizations, the threats to well-being were mostly *sins of omission*, or steps the organizations did not take to center well-being. For example, few experienced any mentoring, programming, or information on how to deal with compassion fatigue or activist burnout from their organizations. Even mentioning feeling burned out in some organizations was met with judgments about one's overall commitment to the cause at hand. The "culture of martyrdom" seemed common across student activist narratives (Gorski & Chen, 2015; Rodgers, 2010). Some students felt isolated even within their activist organizations as if they were the only one experiencing burnout. Others mentioned strained relationships that emerged based on differences of opinion about organizational strategies, leadership, and tactics, as stress inducing. Participants described feeling so overwhelmed at times that their only course of action was to withdraw from their activism.

Conversely, when participants shared the negative effects of college and university actions on their well-being, they most frequently described *sins of commission*, or actions the institution actively took that damaged well-being. The most common complaint among participants was that institutions, and institutional actors such as faculty, staff, and administrators, did not take time to listen to student activists. Even when intentional listening sessions were arranged, activists often came away feeling as if institutional agents were trying to either placate or dismiss their concerns, were intent on defending and maintaining the status quo, or were hoping to wait them out until graduation (Conner, 2020; Ropers-Huilman et al., 2005). College and university leaders were also indicted by study participants for communicating in ways that were oppositional to their stated educational mission and values. Students commonly expressed initial excitement that their institution of higher education espoused values of equity, inclusion, and active citizenship, only to be disappointed when their change-making efforts were met with silence, resistance, or even overt hostility.

Fortunately, these negative effects of organizational and institutional communities on activist well-being were only part of the story. Across our study, we also heard many empowering narratives by students whose psychological, emotional, and physical well-being was bolstered by their communities. Many described the feeling of camaraderie and spoke to the friendships developed through their association with activist organizations. Research has shown that this type of relational reciprocity can build resistance to stress (Ozbay et al., 2007). Some participants described the value of recognition—of both individual and organizational accomplishments—as essential to their own feelings of being valued and motivated. Some activist communities were intentional in offering stress-release activities such as exercise classes, movie nights, dances, and other opportunities to let off steam. Participants shared stories of activist organizations that were very intentional in offering programming describing the dangers of burnout and offering strategies to build resilience, mindfulness, and well-being.

Though fewer in number across our narratives, some students did describe their university community as supportive of activist well-being. This perception is important as a study by Barnhardt and colleagues (2015) revealed that students' commitment to and skills for contributing to the larger community are largely influenced by the extent to which students perceive their campus as one that advocates for its students to be active and involved citizens.

Ropers-Huilman and colleagues (2005) described a range of administrative responses to student activists—from gatekeepers, antagonists, absentee leaders, to supporters. Study participants described experiences where higher education personnel actively reached out to and mentored student activists; where student concerns were heard and students were treated as equal partners in decision making; where curricula and coursework invited praxis and active discussions across differences; where institutional hires included student input and reflected commitments to social justice and equity.

These specific examples of how activist and educational communities can further constrain or empower student activist well-being are an important link between individual and collective care-taking. Even a resilient individual can experience degraded well-being when embedded in toxic or hostile communities and microsystems. Conversely, activists prone to burnout can be bolstered by supportive and responsive activist organizations and institutions of higher education. The next section examines how policy decisions and systemic forces can promote or hinder activist well-being.

Exosystems, Macrosystems, and the Chronosystem: Activist Embeddedness and Paths to Liberation

Beyond the effects of individuals and communities, student activists are also subject to systemic forces. Bronfenbrenner (1992) terms these the exosystem, the macrosystem, and the chronosystem. The exosystem refers to indirect, but powerful influences such as institutional policies, the media, education, laws, and more. The macrosystem encompasses social and cultural values, customs, legal, and economic structures, among others. The chronosystem is the outermost layer of Bronfenbrenner's ecological model and encompasses all of the developmental changes and environmental forces that occur across one's lifespan and in the context of time. Our study revealed key insights about how these forces empower and constrain student activist well-being.

Student activists are typically subject to institutional policies and procedures that may have been designed to support and protect students but can actually function to limit or silence their agency. Conner (2020) described the neoliberal university as a powerful unseen force that could inhibit student well-being. Policies that treat students as consumers, or that prioritize stability over needed changes—especially related to institutional histories of colonization and racism—can be corrosive to well-being. Additionally, public and private institutions of higher education may have different purviews over student activists.

At public universities, free speech is protected but may not be at private colleges. Broadhurst and Martin's (2014) research revealed that students' campus activism was often responsive to the tone and receptiveness they received from campus administrators. The exosystem on university campuses communicates explicit and implicit messages to student activists. Examples of especially egregious messages to student activists include refusing to meet with student activists, rapidly changing or making additions to existing policies in reaction to current protests, and delaying or denying graduation for students who engage in civil disobedience. Quaye and colleagues (2021) wisely cautioned, "the more institutional leaders resist student activists, the more activists will use disruptive tactics in their activism" (p. 113). Thus, a harmful exosystem might actually feed increasingly disruptive activism, which, in turn, can foster increased hostility and backlash against student activists, resulting in even more cases of activist burnout and withdrawal.

When the well-being of college student activists is compromised by negative systemic messages and restrictive university policies, activists may experience enhanced negative affect and heightened emotions such as stress, anger, and frustration (McCarron et al., 2024). At its worst, students can experience the phenomenon of institutional betrayal where wrongdoings perpetrated by institutional agents upon individuals dependent on that institution can result in pragmatic and psychological harm (Smith & Freyd, 2014). The long-term effects of institutional betrayal on student mental health are only now being studied but seem to be correlated with a negative impact on students' academic performance, mental health, identification and engagement with the university, as well as likelihood of future affiliation and donations (Adams-Clark & Freyd, 2021). Institutions seeking to atone for incidents of betrayal should take key steps to acknowledge harm done, to eliminate further incidents, and to center the needs of students.

Each of the layers of Bronfenbrenner's (1992) ecological model are encompassed within the chronosystem, which accounts for both normal developmental and life transitions such as marriage, childbirth, and graduations, as well as non-normative events such as wars, calamities, and the ongoing evolution of technology. Our research team agrees that one of the significant findings of our study is that both activism and well-being are not discrete, static events, but rather they are longitudinal and developmental experiences that take place across space and time. Chapter Three of this volume reminds us that student activists exist in the chronosystem: they visit, revise, reject, and return to the many facets of well-being. Taken together, the exosystem, the macrosystem, and the chronosystem are systemic and socializing forces acting upon student activists.

Harro (2013a) developed a cycle of socialization to depict why it is so hard to counteract the forces of socialization. Harro describes how it can feel impossible to counteract the messages, rules, roles, structures, and assumptions that surround us, as there are enforcements in place to maintain the system. For example, activists who challenge institutional policies or who demand to be part of decision-making structures are often labeled as troublemakers, and may experience discrimination or even violence. So how can activists like those who participated in our study resist or shape the exo- and macrosystems? Harro's (2013b) companion model, the cycle of liberation, offers one path. Harro suggests that most people enter the cycle of liberation as a result of a critical incident that invites them to look at themselves and the world in a new way, called "waking up." For student activists this could come after they notice or experience an institutional or systemic injustice. The next phase of the cycle involves "getting ready" by engaging in important processes such as introspection, education, and consciousness raising, as well as seeking to dismantle stereotypes and discriminatory or privileged attitudes. Each of these phases can be nurtured or disrupted by the institutional and systemic forces of the macro- and exosystems.

As change never happens in isolation, the next phases involve "reaching out," "building community," and "coalescing" with others. Building community involves dialoguing with people who are similar (who share the same social identities, or similar commitments to a cause) and with people who are different from us. For student activists, this may be the most difficult stage. Across the narratives in our study, participants described efforts to reach across ideological borders to engage with representatives of divergent beliefs, with varied effects. Harro (2013a) noted that: "We will never be able to focus on the real challenge—changing the system—until the barriers and boundaries that divide us are minimized" (p. 622). It is a radical act to spend time exploring our differences and deeply listening to those with whom we might initially disagree, yet it may be the only way to create more compassionate systems that center healing and well-being.

According to Harro (2013a), the ultimate goal for most activists is creating systemic change, referring to the process of critically transforming institutions and creating new culture. This stage asks participants to demonstrate leadership, question assumptions, take risks, share power, influence policy, and guide change. Student activists may engage a variety of levers for change, including educating, fundraising, lobbying, conducting action research, working on policy, activism, and allyship (Iowa and Minnesota Campus Compact [IMCC], n.d.). Harro reminds us that making change happen is not the last step in the cycle of liberation; rather, it is "maintenance." It can be even harder to nurture and maintain new structures, rules, roles, and assumptions when life events intervene such as those described in the chronosystem. This step involves more than just organizational work. Our study showcased student activists doing this work through modeling authenticity, integrity, and wholeness. We heard examples of how students spread hope and inspiration across their communities, as well as accepted accountability. Even in tackling seemingly intractable exo-, macro-, and chrono-systemic forces, student activists elucidated the necessity of self- and collective care for fostering well-being in themselves and their communities.

Implications

Our study aimed to contribute to the ongoing discourse and inform actions that promote the well-being and effectiveness of student activists, while advancing positive social change. Through months of listening to, transcribing, and thematizing 119 student narratives, we emerge hopeful that students, activist communities, and institutions of higher education, become more fluent in how to actively promote student activist well-being. This concluding section suggests implications for practice, policy, pedagogy, and further research.

Implications for Practice

Woven throughout this volume are numerous ideas for practically addressing student activist well-being. Here we return to Diener's (2009) model of subjective well-being (SWB). Individuals and communities can promote activist well-being by centering "pleasant emotions" such as joy, contentment, and happiness. Study participants described positive experiences derived from socializing, engaging in artistic endeavors, watching movies, and simply being part of a community outside their activist work. Our research adds to extant research about how to minimize the SWB model's list of "unpleasant emotions" such as sadness, anger, worry, and stress. Individual students detailed numerous actions they took to "unhook" from anxiety and stress invited by their activism, including working out, taking walks, listening to music, and reaching out to peers and supportive educators.

A logical finding of our study is that intentionally learning about wellness and practicing mindfulness invited a stronger cultivation of well-being. Another important insight was the complex interplay of identity, intersectionality, the many vectors of oppression, and well-being. Especially for activists holding marginalized identities, attacks on their well-being felt particularly personal. As described in Chapter Three, understanding the nuances of identity, activism, and well-being is essential to engendering constructive dialogues and reflexive practice across institutions of higher education that center the "student" in college student activism and aim to engage students in the learning journey toward purpose and meaningful aims. For institutions of higher education, we recommend adopting the SOFAR model that elucidates relations between students (S), organization representatives (O), faculty (F), administrators (A), and residents (R) (Bringle et al., 2009). Developed to enhance campus–community partnerships focused on civic engagement, the model allows for a nuanced mapping of the partnerships necessary to make change. The quality of these partnerships is assessed by the degree to which the interactions possess closeness, equity, and integrity, and the degree to which the outcomes of those interactions are exploitive, transactional, or transformational.

In examining the life judgments and domain satisfaction aspects of Diener's (2009) SWB model, we can see the direct links between student activist well-being and feelings of satisfaction, meaning, fulfillment, and success. There is more to explore about how activism itself may be a form of meaning-making that promotes resilience and well-being, as well as the overlaps between the domain satisfaction aspect of the SWB model and Bronfenbrenner's (1996) chronosystem. Additionally, activist communities are waking up to the fact that intentional programming and support for well-being are vital. Several participants describe their organizations hosting self-care awareness sessions, mental health talks, and authentic discussions about how to avoid or address activist burnout. These practical steps can bolster student activists' feelings of value and community and have a prophylactic effect on well-being.

Implications for Policy and Pedagogy

Chapter Five of this volume explored the relationship between university communities, policies, educators, and student activist well-being. It did not surprise us that participants expressed frustration with institutional responses to their activism, and that the barriers and bureaucracy of institutional structures detracted from student activist well-being. The list of institutional roadblocks described was long and included: Colleges being non-responsive to student requests for change; responding to change efforts in superficial or mitigative ways rather than making real transformation; and employing delay tactics designed to push decision making to break periods or even to draw out decision making until activists have graduated or new issues have supplanted old requests for change. Participants lamented the chasm between campus espoused values and actual policies, behaviors, and responses. In fact, this incongruence is highlighted in the scholarship (Quaye et al., 2020). Participants wanted universities to live out the values they publicly proclaim, including one participant's bold suggestion that campuses develop formalized policies and programs focusing on the well-being of students.

Our study revealed other ideas for how institutions could better support the well-being of activists. Participants suggested facilitating student activist organizations in transferring knowledge across leadership and academic transitions; including more student representation in decision making; enhanced flexibility in institutional structures; more access to psychological services and well-being programs; providing safe space for gatherings of student activists; and an overwhelming call for university leaders to spend more time listening to and communicating transparently with students. Several participants called for institutions to value student voices as much as administrators value donors, alumni, and board members. As described in Chapter Five, it seems a simple request from student activists—to be listened to, taken seriously, and acknowledged for their efforts to try and make institutions of higher education to be more just, equitable, and inclusive spaces.

We also heard numerous narratives about the value of participating in courses and undergraduate research across disciplines that addressed student activism, well-being, and social issues. This seems especially timely given the attacks on and erosion of these kinds of programs at U.S. institutions. Chapter Two describes the salience of High-Impact Practices (HIPs), especially civic and community engagement, in fostering reciprocal and non-extractive forms of activism. It should be noted that research shows HIPs have a positive differential impact for students holding minoritized identities, yet also reveals these students are less frequently engaged in HIPs at colleges and universities (Finley & McNair, 2013). Overall, our research supports the recent calls from higher education scholars, administrators, and foundations to revive the civic mission of colleges and universities (Institute for Democracy and Higher Education [IDHE], 2024; Weerts et al., 2014). Direct actions such as promoting voter engagement, addressing public problems, and promoting dialogues across ideological differences, are just a few of the examples of campus-wide efforts to reverse the decline (Institute for Democracy and Higher Education [IDHE], 2024; National Task Force on Civic Learning and Democratic Engagement, 2012).

Implications for Further Research

There are a wealth of implications from our study for further research. Overall, we found that the literature linking student activism and well-being to be underdeveloped and in need of additional complexity. Extant scholarship seemed to fall into two categories. One category features studies heralding the many benefits of activism on student agency and development, including the development of identity, intellectual development, democratic skills, and leadership skills such as organizing, critical thinking, effective communication, and working across differences. A second and somewhat larger category, were studies that decried the deleterious effects of activism on well-being. As detailed in Chapter Four of this volume, this research reveals three primary signs of activist burnout: (1) exhaustion (feeling emotionally and physically drained); (2) cynicism (developing negative perceptions of once-significant work); and (3) inefficacy (doubting one's self-worth and perceiving a lack of activist accomplishments) (Maslach & Gomes, 2006). We suggest future scholarship go beyond viewing student activism as inherently beneficial or deleterious to student well-being, and instead seek multiplicity and complexity. For example, emergent scholarship from Grande and Staton (in press) suggests the most efficacious way to foster authentic hope in student activists is to intentionally pair an acknowledgment of the challenges of sustaining hope with the knowledge, skills, and behaviors to address these challenges. The few recent meta-analytic studies of student activism were adroit at weaving the complex narrative of activist engagement and burnout (Linder et al., 2020; Quaye et al., 2021).

As a research team, we hope the research and practice implications of our findings will be applied across numerous disciplines, including social justice, human rights, leadership studies, and higher education. By doing so, we aim to contribute to the ongoing discourse and inform actions that promote the well-being and effectiveness of student activists, while advancing positive social change. We are energized to leverage student development theory to map how students' affective and cognitive complexity might shape which types of well-being approaches are most efficacious. Additionally, future research might take a longitudinal approach to exploring how college student activists' identities shape their sense of purpose, fulfillment, meaning, and other life judgments. Regardless of the nature of scholarly work, the aim should be consistent: Fostering knowledge that helps college student activists fortify the bridge between who they are and what they do.

Conclusion

There are major forces impacting colleges and universities that promise to transform the higher education sector (Alexander, 2020). From economic uncertainty and legislative intrusion to the advent of artificial intelligence and climate change, these ominous trends make the work of higher education administrators, staff, and faculty members daunting. In this context the idea of responding to student protests would seemingly be met as one more challenge on top of an already overflowing list of concerns. We do not disagree that responding to student demands, holding difficult dialogues, rethinking policies, reconsidering the status quo, and answering calls from disgruntled stakeholders could be unenviable. The mission of higher education is unique though—we are charged with preparing graduates to take on the most vexing challenges facing society. Constructing environments where students learn the complex skills of being active members of a democracy, such as working across differences to make social change, means that faculty and staff will have to engage in this messy work to help our institutions live up to our lofty ideals and aspirations. Recognizing the ecological embeddedness in which all these actions occur, is also imperative if well-being supports are to be efficacious (Bronfenbrenner, 1977, 1996).

Student activism leads to the outcomes that most campuses seek. When students advocate for equity, inclusion, and fairness on their campus they are not only demonstrating care, but they are also helping their institution improve. There are countless examples where student protest demands eventually led to new programs, initiatives, and commitments that would make colleges and universities more welcoming. However, not all students arrive on campus fully formed. We implore our colleagues to use a developmental approach that respects students' growing awareness of the complexity of issues, while simultaneously respecting student insights and creativity (Owen et al., 2022).

Supporting the subjective well-being of student activists through the practices outlined throughout this text, by pursuing the policy objectives described above, or conducting research into related experiences and constructs, contributes to our most important role: Achieving our mission.

References

Adams-Clark, A. A., & Freyd, J. J. (2021). COVID-19-related institutional betrayal associated with trauma symptoms among undergraduate students. *PLOS ONE, 16*(10). https://doi.org/10.1371/journal.pone.0258294

Alexander, B. (2020). *Academia next: The futures of higher education.* Johns Hopkins University Press.

Barnhardt, C. L., Sheets, J. E., & Pasquesi, K. (2015). You expect what? Students' perceptions as resources in acquiring commitments and capacities for civic engagement. *Research in Higher Education, 56*, 622–644. https://doi.org/10.1007/s11162-014-9361-8

Bringle, R. G., Clayton, P. H., & Price, M. (2009). Partnerships in service learning and civic engagement. *Partnerships: A Journal of Service Learning & Civic Engagement, 1*(1), 1–20. https://doi.org/10.7253/partj.v1i1.415

Broadhurst, C., & Martin, G. L. (2014). Part of the "establishment"? Fostering positive campus climates for student activists. *Journal of College and Character, 15*(2), 75–86. https://doi.org/10.1515/jcc-2014-0012

Bronfenbrenner, U. (1977). Toward an experimental ecology of human development. *American Psychologist, 32*(7), 513–531. https://doi.org/10.1037/0003-066X.32.7.513

Bronfenbrenner, U. (1992). Ecological systems theory. In R. Vasta (Ed.), *Six theories of child development: Revised formulations and current issues* (pp. 187–249). Jessica Kingsley Publishers.

Bronfenbrenner, U. (1993). The ecology of cognitive development: Research models and fugitive findings. In R. H. Wozniak & K. W. Fischer (Eds.), *Development in context: Acting and thinking in specific environments* (pp. 3–44). Erlbaum.

Bronfenbrenner, U. (1996). *The ecology of human development experiments by nature and design*. Harvard University Press.

Conner, J. O. (2020). *The new student activists: The rise of neoactivism on college campuses*. Johns Hopkins University Press.

Diener, E. (2009). Subjective well-being. In E. Diener (Ed.), *The Science of well-being: The collected works of Ed Diener* (pp. 11–58). Springer. https://doi.org/10.1007/978-90-481-2350-6_2

Ellison, B., & Braxton, J. M. (2023). Reviewing, theorizing, and looking ahead: The relationships between college students' sense of belong and persistence. In E. Bentrim & G. W. Henning (Eds.), *The impact of a sense of belonging in college: Implications for student persistence, retention, and success* (pp. 35–56). Taylor & Francis.

Evans, M., & Fisher, E. B. (2022). Social isolation and mental health: The role of nondirective and directive social support. *Community Mental Health Journal*, *58*, 20–40. https://doi.org/10.1007/s10597-021-00787-9

Finley, A., & McNair, T. (2013). *Assessing underserved students' engagement in high-impact practices*. Association of American Colleges and Universities. www.aacu.org/publication/assessing-underserved-students-engagement-in-high-impact-practices

Gay, R. (2022). *Inciting joy*. Algonquin books.

Gervais, M. (2023). *The first rule of mastery: Stop worrying about what people think of you*. Harvard Business Press.

Gorski, P. C., & Chen, C. (2015). "Frayed all over:" The causes and consequences of activist burnout among social justice education activists. *Educational Studies: Journal of the American Educational Studies Association*, *51*(5), 385–405. https://doi.org/10.1080/00131946.2015.1075989

Grande, S. E., & Staton, A. R. (In press). Authentic hope in troubling times. *New Directions in Teaching and Learning*.

Harro, B. (2013a). The cycle of liberation. In M. Adams, W. J. Blumenfeld, R. Castaneda, H. W. Hackman, M. L. Peters, & X. Zuñiga (Eds.), *Readings for diversity and social justice* (3rd Ed., pp. 618–625). Routledge.

Harro, B. (2013b). The cycle of socialization. In M. Adams, W. J. Blumenfeld, R. Castaneda, H. W. Hackman, M. L. Peters, & X. Zuñiga (Eds.), *Readings for diversity and social justice* (3rd Ed., pp. 45–52). Routledge.

Institute for Democracy and Higher Education (IDHE). (2024). *Democracy re/designed*. American Association of Colleges & Universities (AAC&U).

www.aacu.org/initiatives/institute-for-democracy-and-higher-education/redesigning-democracy

Iowa and Minnesota Campus Compact (IMCC). (n.d.). Social change wheel 2.0 toolkit. https://seed-coalition.org/wp-content/uploads/2024/06/Social-Change-Wheel-2.0-Toolkit-05.08.2021.pdf

Linder, C., Quaye, S. J., Lange, A. C., Evans, M. E., & Stewart, T. J. (2020). *Identity-based student activism: Power and oppression on college campuses*. Routledge.

Maslach, C., & Gomes, M. E. (2006). Overcoming burnout. In R. M. MacNair (Ed.), *Working for peace: A handbook of practical psychology and other tools* (2nd Ed., pp. 43–49). Impact Publishers.

McCarron, G. P., Chen, C. W., April, J., & LaMagdeleine, I. (2024). An exploratory study of the relationship between college student activists' labor and their subjective well-being: Perspectives from a U.S. institution. *Journal of American College Health*, 1–10. Online First. https://doi.org/10.1080/07448481.2024.2338409

McCarron, G. P., Chen, C. W., Blanton, S., Guerrieri, G., Lucioni, R. G., Gurung, E., Sreevals, A., & Enciu, J. (2023). College student activists' perceptions of mattering to campus educators. *Journal of Student Affairs Research and Practice*, *61*(3), 368–384. https://doi.org/10.1080/19496591.2023.2201195

National Task Force on Civic Learning and Democratic Engagement. (2012). *A crucible moment: College learning and democracy's future*. Association of American Colleges and Universities. www.aacu.org/civic learning/crucible/index.cfm

Nicolazzo, Z. (2016). "Just go in looking good:" The resilience, resistance, and kinship-building of Trans college students. *Journal of College Student Development*, *57*(5), 538–556. https://doi.org/10.1353/csd.2016.0057

Owen, J. E., McCarron, G. P., & Chen, C. (2022). "Never 'because of', always 'in spite of'": Implications of the Culturally-Relevant Leadership Learning Model for student social justice activists' leadership learning. *Journal of Leadership Studies*, *16*(3), 45–50. https://doi.org/10.1002/jls.21820

Ozbay, F., Johnson D. C., Dimoulas, E., Morgan, C. A., Charney, D., & Southwick, S. (2007). Social support and resilience to stress: From neurobiology to clinical practice. *Psychiatry*, *4*(5), 35–40. PMID: 20806028.

Pierce, J. E. (2021). *Belonging through dissent: A national study of student activist sense of belonging and institutional integration* (Publication No. 28411444) [Doctoral dissertation, University of Georgia].

Quaye, S. J., Lange, A. C., Benbow, R. J., Pfund, C., Thayer-Hart, N., & Branchaw, J. (2020). Pete's letter: A student activist's message to campus administrators. *Journal of Diversity in Higher Education*, *13*(3), 240–253. https://doi.org/10.1037/dhe0000293

Quaye, S. J., Linder, C., Stewart, T. J., & Satterwhite, E. M. (2021). A critical examination of college student activism from 2000–2020. In L. W. Perna

(Ed.), *Higher education: Handbook of theory and research* (pp. 81–132). Springer.

Renn, K. A., & Arnold, K. D. (2003). Reconceptualizing research on college student peer culture. *Journal of Higher Education, 74*(3), 261–291. https://doi.org/10.1353/jhe.2003.0025

Rodgers, K. (2010). "Anger is why we're all here:" Mobilizing and managing emotions in a professional activist organization. *Social Movement Studies, 9*, 273–291. https://doi.org/10.1080/14742837.2010.493660

Ropers-Huilman, B., Carwile, L., & Barnett, K. (2005). Student activists' characterizations of administrators in higher education: Perceptions of power in "the system." *The Review of Higher Education, 28*(3), 295–312. https://doi.org/10.1353/rhe.2005.0012

Smith, C. P., & Freyd, J. J. (2014). Institutional betrayal. *American Psychologist, 69*(6), 575–587. https://doi.org/10.1037/a0037564

Soloman, A. (2014, March). *How the worst moments in our lives make us who we are* [Video]. TED: Ideas change everything. www.ted.com/talks/andrew_solomon_how_the_worst_moments_in_our_lives_make_us_who_we_are/transcript?subtitle=en

Warnock, D. M., & Hurst, A. L. (2016). "The poor kids' table:" Organizing around an invisible and stigmatized identity in flu. *Journal of Diversity in Higher Education, 9*(3), 261–276. https://doi.org/10.1037/dhe0000029

Weerts, D. J., Cabrera, A. F., & Mejías, P. P. (2014). Uncovering categories of civically engaged college students: A latent class analysis. *Review of Higher Education, 37*(2), 141–168. https://doi.org/10.1353/rhe.2014.0008

Index

For Product Safety Concerns and Information please contact our EU
representative GPSR@taylorandfrancis.com
Taylor & Francis Verlag GmbH, Kaufingerstraße 24, 80331 München, Germany

www.ingramcontent.com/pod-product-compliance
Lightning Source LLC
LaVergne TN
LVHW010917110826
845149LV00013B/2399
* 9 7 8 1 0 3 2 7 7 0 4 9 9 *